THE SACRAMENT
OF
LOVE

PAUL EVDOKIMOV

THE SACRAMENT OF LOVE

The Nuptial Mystery in the Light
of the Orthodox Tradition

Translated from the French
by
ANTHONY P. GYTHIEL and VICTORIA STEADMAN

with a foreword
by
OLIVIER CLEMENT

ST VLADIMIR'S SEMINARY PRESS
CRESTWOOD, NY 10707
1985

Published under the title
SACREMENT DE L'AMOUR
by Desclée de Brouwer, Paris 1980

Library of Congress Cataloging in Publication Data

Evdokimov, Paul, 1901-1970.
    The sacrament of love.

    Translation of: Sacrement de l'amour.
    Includes bibliographies.
    1. Marriage—Religious aspects—Orthodox Eastern
Church.   2. Orthodox Eastern Church—Doctrines.   I.   Title.
BX378.M2E9313   1985   234'.165   85-2261
ISBN 0-88141-042-X

THE SACRAMENT OF LOVE

This Translation © Copyright 1985

by

ST VLADIMIR'S SEMINARY PRESS

ISBN 0-88141-042-X

PRINTED IN THE UNITED STATES OF AMERICA
BY
ATHENS PRINTING COMPANY
NEW YORK, NY

Contents

FOREWORD 7

INTRODUCTION 15
   Historical Background 19
   Two Key Concepts 22
   The Myths 28
   The Charisms Of Woman 31
   The Mother 32
   Woman: Spiritual Instrument of Human Nature 34
   Woman: Point of Encounter Between God and Man .. 37
   The Personalistic Conception of Marriage 41
   The Ultimate Light 46

1. ANTHROPOLOGY 49
   The Hour of Witnesses 49
   The Philanthropy of God 50
   The Constitution of the Human Being:
      The Spirit and the Flesh 50
   The Biblical Concept of the Heart 51
   The Human Person 53
   Freedom 55
   The Image and Likeness of God 58
   The Disease and the Cure 59
   The Liturgical Vocation of Man 61

2. MARRIAGE AND THE MONASTIC STATE 65
   The One Absolute 65
   The Calling 69
   Monasticism 73
   The Ascetic Monasticism of Every Believer 81
   Universal Interiorized Monasticism 83

3. THE ROYAL PRIESTHOOD OF THE BELIEVERS 85
   The Functional Priesthood of Ordination and the
      Ontological Priesthood of the Believers 85

The Sacrament of the Anointing with
    Chrism and its Three Dignities 87
The New Holiness 92
Nonmonastic Celibacy 95

4. LOVE AND THE SACRAMENT OF LOVE 105
The Harmonics of Love 105
The Prophetic Revelations and the Eternal Present 111
The Image of God 115
The Proper Aim of Marriage 119
The Domestic Church 121
The Sacraments 123
The Paradisiac Institution 125
The Paradisiacal Institution 125
Joy 127
The Minister of the Sacrament 128
The Sacrament of Marriage in the Byzantine Rite 130
Brief Commentary on the Sacrament of Marriage 148

5. SEXUALITY AND NUPTIAL CHASTITY 161
The Problem 161
The Modern Myth of Sexuality 164
Chastity 168
Birth Control: The Problem of Limiting Births 174

6. THE INSTITUTION 181
Marriage in Eastern Canon Law 181
The Canonical Status of Marriage 183
Married Love and Divorce 186

The translators, Anthony P. Gythiel and Victoria
Steadman, acknowledge with gratitude the assistance
they received from the English Department and the
Graduate School at Wichita State University, Kansas.

Foreword

The Sacrament of Love is but one panel (the second being *Woman and the Salvation of the World* [Paris, 1978]) of the diptych that Paul Evdokimov dedicated to the spiritual gifts of men and women and to the sacramental "mystery" of human love.

It would be trite to say that the erotic has hardly found a place in the history of Christianity except, fully transformed, in the spiritual outcome of monasticism. Christianity has fought to maintain the transcendence of the person against the blind impulse of the species and the idolatry of impersonal pleasure. This transcendence is achieved in the mystic union, where "desire returns to its origin," as St Gregory Palamas says. Nonetheless, the monastic tension between the person and nature has often become distention, where an entire dualistic sensibility and a disembodied spirituality are engulfed. Hence the dream of an asexual or "angelic" condition, the fear of the woman, the patent unease of many a Church Father over the passage in Genesis commemorating the extraordinary encounter between man and woman in Paradise before the Fall. Some of them have gone so far as to say that it was precisely in view of the Fall and also to assure the history of salvation that God created woman. Or else they detected in the very intensity of erotic pleasure the insurmountable beginning of death—a profound observation, but one that forgets both the condition in Paradise and the first miracle of Christ at the wedding of Cana. It would appear that during the Christian era entire sections of the Gospel have been buried, even denied—the liberating freedom of Christ toward the most "impure" or the most "sinful" women according to the Law and the reminder He makes of the original

7

intention of the Creator, of the initial "consubstantiality" of
man and woman, "they shall be one flesh." Such a reminder
does not involve a new law, from the legalistic perspective,
but a meaning, an attraction, a grace offered again. Suffice it
to think of the prohibitions, at once unpolished and salacious,
of the "penitentials" in the East as well as in the West, or of
the frequently dreadful punishment of the adulteress ("Let
him who has never sinned cast the first stone") and one will
understand the modern revolt against what has been taken
for the Christian concept of sexuality . . .

It should be said that in the Christian era there is not much
difference in this domain between the various Churches.
However, in the second half of the last century and the first
of the present, the Orthodox Church has offered a favorable
climate for a renewed awareness of the spiritual value of
human love, because it has kept the married priesthood of
the early centuries (whereas in the West the horror of sex,
and especially of woman, resulted in mandatory celibacy for
the clergy, which today, though, is justified differently). The
Orthodox Church has also tempered legalism by the concept
of "economy," that is, out of respect for the destiny of each
person. However, let us not be mistaken. This reflection did
not come solely from traditional Orthodoxy, but from the
encounter in Russia between men on the one hand who had
experienced Western modernity, its dead ends but also its
demands, and a Church on the other hand that they had freely
joined as adults, laymen who frequently had experienced
tragedy in life but who were fully determined to seek what is
essential while thrusting aside the clerical and pious forms of
Pharisaism. It appears to me that it is these Russian religious
philosophers who were the first in the Christian world to
have sensed the spiritual meaning of Eros and who began to
surmount the deadly schism that had inserted itself between
human love and Christianity. These men, who were also great
Western intellectuals, carried within themselves this expectation of a love appropriately personal, free, and reciprocal,
the expectation that characterizes modernity and painfully
opens up a path between the ultimately hedonistic myth of
Don Juan and the myth of the ultimate dissolution of Tristan

and Isolde, between freedom without love and love without freedom. This Russian reflection was abundant and complex, often contradictory. Leaving aside the poets (whose quest and intuitions were crystallized in Pasternak's admirable *Doctor Zhivago*), let us at least mention some of the religious philosophers: Bukharev and his decision to give up monastic orders in order to marry and live humbly among men; Soloviev and Bulgakov who discover the femininity of creation, indeed the femininity of God, through the symbol of "Sophia," and dream of a love that is deeply personal yet free of all carnal expression; Rozanov who, with Biblical overtones that oppose him to the monastic tradition, extols the cult of the body as the language of faithfulness; Berdyaev, for whom true love shatters all social and ecclesiastical objectifications and anticipates the transfiguration of the world, but which only has meaning in freedom; Vysheslavstev who replaces the Freudian obsession with the sexual by the "ethics of the transfigured Eros" . . .

It is the heritage of this research that we find in Evdokimov, an inheritance that he accepted upon verification and the perceptions of which he was able to bring into play within the context of modern Europe (using, for example, not the system of Jung, but only its symbolism).

In *Woman and the Salvation of the World* the vocations proper to man and woman are outlined through two languages: a Trinitarian language, since the human being is in the image of God, the masculine on the whole reflecting the *Logos* and the feminine the *Pneuma,* and a Christ-centered language, since Christ recapitulates all humanity, the masculine finding its archetype in John the Baptist (and his lineage, from Elijah to the witnesses of Revelation), the feminine in the Theotokos and the Woman clothed with the sun.

In *The Sacrament of Love* (this title was created by St John Chrysostom, one of the few Church Fathers whose pastoral concerns and scriptural sense led to a valuation of human love), Paul Evdokimov bases his thesis on the two accounts of the creation of man and woman in Genesis—accounts that Christ draws together in order to show simultaneously in the couple unity and otherness. To borrow from a profound

Jewish exegesis, God created the human (*ha adam*) male and female. Taking not a rib, but a half of this reality still not fully differentiated, He places the woman facing the man. This is the discovery of another person who is nonetheless consubstantial to me ("bone of my bone and flesh of my flesh"). The theological correspondences are obvious, and Evdokimov has no trouble bringing them to light: the mystery of the Trinity, the inaccessible God who makes Himself accessible. In its original fullness, human love reflects the Communion of the Trinity; the otherness of God is the foundation for the otherness of the other, and His grace is the basis for the encounter.

Evdokimov, however, knows life and knows the lucid diagnosis of the ascetics too well to be carried away by lyricism. He shows that the separation of God has led, and leads, to separation from the other. The distinction in the unity of the man and the woman is turned into a "battle of the sexes," even more unforgiving because the proximity of Paradise constantly experienced, constantly lost, leaves man and woman even more disenchanted with each other. The enslavement of woman, her revenge and the fascination that she exerts, the demonization of the feminine, the "fusional" gnoses that Scripture abhors, are so many aspects of the present situation of Eros. Evdokimov, who is often ironic in this book, questions the Western concept of "natural law." Polygamy was "natural" for the Old Testament patriarchs just as it is today in Islam. Polyandry was "natural" in Tibet. In the nineteenth century, prostitution gave the most "natural" balance to the monogamous puritanism of the bourgeois family.

Only Christ, Evdokimov argues, can truly reconcile man and woman and bring about the harmony of Eros and the person. *The Sacrament of Love* reconciles the two sayings of the Apostle: "In Christ there is neither male nor female" and "In Christ woman is not without man, neither man without woman." Each is viewed in the full dignity of a person, independent of one's defined function. At the same time, the nuptial consubstantiality is reestablished, and the two poles take their place in the full image of God.

From this perspective, there is no need to defend the

mystery of marriage; it carries its own justification. It regulates nothing, except the communion between man and woman in all its sacramental fullness. "It is from this overflowing fullness," Evdokimov writes, "that the child can come as a fruit, but it is not procreation that determines and establishes the value of marriage." True love is fruitful. But this fruitfulness is not only expressed through the child; it can also be manifested through hospitality, through service, and sometimes through a common creation.

In the misery and disorder of our lives, true love thus demands—like monasticism, but in a more humble and apparently more prosaic way—asceticism and sanctification. Moreover, it implies, with man as with woman, an "interiorized monasticism" (another fundamental theme for Evdokimov), the healthy solitude that each must respect in the other in order to keep alive the sense of one's otherness. At times, only distance allows one to perceive the unity; only an awareness that the more the other is known the more he is unknown creates the deepening and the renewal of love.

This asceticism of human love finds its full meaning in the concept of chastity, so important to the Russian religious philosophers. Chastity does not necessarily mean continence; it signifies the integrity and wholeness of the spirit, of the heart-spirit assuming all the power of life, of Eros, in the encounter with a person, which makes the body no longer an object but the poetry of a true tenderness. The body's language would be an incomprehensible and heart-rending cry if it were not claiming true eternity, the one that unfolds with the passage of time, with patience, and with fidelity.

The man and the woman who are engaged in this mystery must know that they will only decipher in the most incomplete fashion the boundless love that goes before them and sustains them, that of Christ and of the Church, of the Communion of the Trinity itself. Through forgiveness, humility and trust, which are deeper than their own frail and unsteady love, it is always (or nearly always) possible for the couple to recapture this inexhaustible depth that will renew their union.

Evdokimov stresses that, in all of this, the Church gives

the meaning and offers the life-giving power of the sacrament, but is not to impose restrictions and panaceas. The Roman Catholic Church has wanted to regulate family planning by forbidding artificial birth control. The Orthodox Church, more than Evdokimov admits, knows similar temptations. In general, though, it exercises the greatest discretion. Advice given is personal, and the "stages" of the married life are taken into account. The Church explains the meaning and the immensity of love, the ascesis and the responsibility that it implies, and it denounces the extreme gravity of abortion. For the rest, the Orthodox Church knows that no one can decide for the couple. The partners are the ones who are important; the quality of their relationship is important, not the methods, which may or may not be "natural." Such discussions among celibate ecclesiastics have something morbid (or something purely comical) about them; the celibate would condescend to the faithful if one did not know that the latter, for quite some time now, have no longer taken any notice. To explain the meaning and leave the rest to the conscience of the spouses, who can find help, should the occasion arise, from a spiritual director—this is the attitude of the Russian Church from which Evdokimov sprang. It is also the position so vigorously affirmed by Patriarch Athenagoras.

It remains true, however, that the historical context has changed and that today Paul Evdokimov, without changing his basic view, would undoubtedly present it differently. For the first time in history, woman has acquired complete control over conception, the control of which, in the atmosphere of contemporary nihilism, threatens important groups of the human race with collective suicide. It would perhaps be more necessary, then, to emphasize the importance and the mystery of the child, the conscious act of faith that now constitutes the "bringing to birth," biologically and spiritually, of this strange guest of the couple.

Finally, Evdokimov reminds us that the Orthodox Church, in its love as mother, does not exclude the divorced from communion and, in certain cases, determines that a marriage does not exist, going so far as to bless subsequent marriages, when they are entered with a spirit of repentance. It is not a question of complacency in this matter, but of a truly evangelical "economy" in the hands of the spiritual men and bishops, and in which the person and his unique destiny go beyond all generalities, all objectification, all legalism. "The Sabbath was made for man and not man for the Sabbath." This perspective is one that the Christian West, so deeply torn by its problems, is beginning to ignore no longer. It is not, we should remember, the attitude of a lax and secularized Church, but of a Church that always puts in the forefront the character of the sacrament and the need for asceticism.

OLIVIER CLEMENT

Introduction

"Have you not read that He who made them from the beginning made them male and female, and said, '. . . man shall . . . be joined to his wife, and the two shall become one flesh'?" To the disciples who said, "If such is the case of a man with his wife, it is not expedient to marry," the Lord replies, "He who is able to receive this, let him receive it" (Mt 19:1-12).

This brief dialogue throws into striking relief the vertiginous distance between the divine order and human institutions. At precisely what moment "that which was in the beginning" turned toward "that which is now" is covered by the mists of time and the "twilight of the idols." We can only follow a series of critical junctures which are at the same time dreadful judgments.

Christianity has raised the nuptial union to the dignity of a sacrament. However, this revolutionary move strikes against a tendency deeply anchored in the general mentality, which considers marriage only from the external viewpoint of sociological usefulness, from the point of view of rights and duties. The mystery of love itself, its hidden dimension which is always unique and personal, remains in the shadow and does not even reach the domain of morals and human customs. A "mental humus," formed through thousands of years, strongly resists the evangelical "metanoia," the "change of heart."

Modern psychology uses the term *über sich* or *superego* to designate the collective consciousness. The latter possesses enormous influence; by means of ancestral atavisms, it bears down with all its weight on each individual consciousness. The archetypes and complexes act with their mysterious charm.

The *superego* keeps watch over the apparent balance of accepted ideas. It expertly thrusts aside all "metanoia" (i.e. change of mind, conversion), having become capable of awakening anguish and pained awareness in the presence of adulterated values. Every spirit that dares run counter to conformity, that wonders whether it belongs to those that "can accept this word" of the Lord, is at once suspect in its orthodoxy. Such is the hypnotic power of all "ancient belief." But the ancient as such is never a valid criterion. It can become petrified in us, who stand in the temporal dimension of what was "in the beginning," in the mind of God ever present and new, in the dimension that transcends time.

On the other hand, the "constraint of repetition" always tries to reproduce the same situations; it creates false myths such as, for example, the masculine myth of virility, of man the generator, the stud. Thus through thousands of years, this constraint has subordinated woman to man, the pair to the necessity of the species, and love to the service of procreation.

The onerous heritage of Antiquity finds an echo in the formation of asceticism. In Essene circles, with the monks of Qumran, the perfect are those who cultivate celibacy. This becomes characteristic of early Judaeo-Christianity. The enthusiastic praise of celibacy by the Syrians, who are somewhat inflexible by nature, becomes a condemnation of marriage, as in Satornilus, Tatian, Marcion, The Gospel of the Egyptians, and later Julius Cassian. Christian thought exalts virginity positively, as a separate value, but does not always remain at this height, turning as it does to the negative aspect, the depreciation of marriage. In its extremist currents, the struggle against the flesh identifies the flesh with concupiscence, then with woman, and advocates the flight from all that is feminine. At times, one has the impression that the problem of salvation is for men alone, and that he who wants to save himself must, above all, save himself from women. There is an echo of Gnosticism in this, where "redemption" means "deliverance from sex" and where woman is reduced to the purely sexual and, from there, to the demonic. A certain type of ascetic even refuses to see his own mother because she is a woman and exhibits disquieting attention to the accursed sex even in the animal world. The Cathari push this encratite[1] asceticism to its limit and declare marriage a satanic abomination.

Surprisingly, it is with the hermits that the "woman question" becomes most current, reducing it to its "passionate" aspect and compromising it forever. Certain theologians deem it useless to propagate the human race; they reduce marriage to the one aim of avoiding incontinence. This is why a conjugal love that is too passionate borders on adultery. On what scale should one weigh passion? Can one gauge the effects of similar calculations on an awakening love, most often chaste, that is free of all eroticism? Only an abstract being can "invent" such restraints and thereby poison with his distrust the dew of a blossoming flower. Women who react to the wishes of a misunderstood asceticism are nowadays identified as "frigid women"; doctors understand the tragedies that this attitude creates in marital intimacy. It renders men impotent or drives them to extramarital substitutions. On the other hand there are those, unhappy because of loneliness, who even with prostitutes look for a simple feminine presence, an illusion of love. In these extreme cases eroticism, sexuality properly understood, is no longer at work . . .

When it is simplistic, the exaltation of virginity borders on paradox. It seems to say that Christianity is defined by celibacy and makes of marriage only a tolerated exception. In the mysterious and irrational element of his being, man sees himself disembodied from his mystery, entirely determined by the most elementary physiology and the most pragmatic sociology. One could say that here the Gospel has not brought any great changes. One readily understands what deep uneasiness can be implanted in a woman's soul, sensitive and attentive, by the many affirmations of the Church's theologians —purely gratuitous affirmations, even though they are the product of spiritual authorities who are otherwise beyond dispute.[2] So much was this so that between the summit of

[1]The Gnostic sect of the "Encratites," that is the "abstinent," rejected marriage as adultery. This group substituted water for wine in the eucharistic service and was called the sect of the "Aquarians." (They flourished in the East around 170 A.D.)

[2]For example, "Woman is the gate of Hell," "The Lord Himself opens

humanity, the Virgin Mary who is "beyond compare more glorious than the Seraphim" and whose praise rises like a single spire, and an incomplete and demonic feminine being, there does not exist, so it appears, a third option. An amazing alienation has established itself in history as a normal situation.

The legally and finalistic principle of Jewish thought penetrates from within and strongly permeates certain Christian thought; the latter sometimes risks "sitting on the seat of Moses" and developing a transposed Rabbinism.[3] On the other hand, Monophysitism,[4] an easy solution, gains the advantage many times and warps the theological consciousness. The theologians of the patristic era center their interest on questions of dogma; monks themselves, and mostly virgins, they had neither the necessary experience nor the time and interest for a philosophy of love. Very rich in ascetical treatises, this era skirts the transphysiological mystery of the sexes. The magnificent heroism of the ascetics unleashed a decisive battle within man himself and exorcised the demonic powers from him, but at a price that verges on the dehumanization of relationships between man and woman. It appears that certain theologians' opinions on married love are taken from zoology manuals; the couple is seen from the viewpoint of reproduction and child-raising. One also finds entire systems that connect "ordination" to "subordination" and "superordination"

'the Kingdoms of the Heavens' to 'eunuchs' " (Tertullian, *On the Dress of Woman; Monogamy* III. 8). St Ambrose states that "married people ought to be ashamed of the state in which they live" (PL 16:346). To Clement of Alexandria, "for woman even to reflect on her nature results in opprobrium" (*Paedogogus*, II. 2, PG 8:429).

[3]In his article titled "L'idée du mariage," in *Etudes Carmélitaines* (1938), B. M. Lavaud writes, "Suffice it to peruse a work like that of P. Browe, S. J., *Beiträge zur Sexualethik des Mittelalters* (Breslau, 1932), to have a notion of the persistence and the diffusion, during the Middle Ages, of rules and practices that can only be explained by an inadequate discernment of the moral and the 'legal' in the Old Testament (temporary removal from the Church, from the divine service, and from the sacraments, removal of the woman after menstruation, of the mother after childbirth, of the spouses after sexual relations, and so forth)," p. 169, note 2. See the study by Dominikus Linder, *Der Usus Matrimonii* (Munich, 1929).

[4]From the Greek *monos*, "one," and *physis*, "nature." The heresy bearing this name confesses that in Christ there is but a single (Divine) nature, which fact thereby suppresses His human nature.

to determine whether man is the chief or the head. The question of love in itself and of its meaning still remains open today and reveals a deep malaise: Scholasticism favors procreation, but castrates love . . .

Historical Background

At a time of salutary reactions to heresies, libertinage, and the laxist tendency, an overvaluation of the sexual was bound to occur in the theological consciousness—in certain cases carried to obsession—accompanied by an undervaluation of marriage. In the heat of polemics balanced thought suffers distortion. With the most pessimistic theoreticians on the subject of the flesh, their conception, for lack of experience, is but a mental view; with the others, an inordinate asceticism replaced an equally inordinate life.

Even today a large number of treatises on marriage are written in the West by monks or celibates; this is why they do not achieve their objective and miss the point. Can one write, except in the case of special revelation, something correct about one's opposite where neither agenda nor resentment, neither illusion nor theory intervenes? It is not appropriate for the married to discourse on the monastic life, nor does it suit the unmarried to construct a phenomenology of Eros. One might regret that it was not the Apostle Peter who wrote on the theme of chapter seven of the First Letter to the Corinthians.

Virgins would certainly be amazed to know that at the time of engagement sexuality is quite simply nonexistent, and that afterward, in married life, it evolves very rapidly and passes to an entirely different plane than the one it continues to occupy in the imagination of virgins. In harmonious unions, where the vision is not distorted by false theories, sexuality undergoes a progressive spiritualization in order to reach conjugal chastity. The flesh is not an element that one can strike from the spirit or reduce to silence. The flesh is the biosphere where the spirit becomes incarnate when offered to its transfiguring powers; indeed, it is the open tomb where the spirit buries itself alive. Augustine says: "He who is not spiritual in his flesh becomes carnal even in his spirit." One can even paraphrase this statement: the one who is not spiritual in his sex becomes sexual even in his spirit. Stopping halfway is a failure that cannot be overlooked and produces the monstrous disorders of a mystic eroticism or of the spirit become flesh.

More than ever and more than anywhere else, clearsightedness and spiritual attentiveness are essential as the true ascetic cultivation proper to the married life. This cultivation is a function of adult human persons who are an end in themselves, always subjects, never objects, because they are the point of intersection between two worlds. This cultivation has nothing to do with the dullness of current catechisms. It struggles against all forms of slavery, and this is why its ethic is totally removed from the law of the "general," from the tyranny of conformity and objectification, from all submission to the "common good," from every necessity of nature as well as of society. Its freedom is not a right, but the royal charter of duty, for it is a response to the call from God. The priestly dignity of man requires it. According to the saying of the Church Fathers, "God only speaks to gods." Such is the will of God. All else is human history.

*   *   *

In Old Testament times, polygamy made it easy to repudiate women. Levirate institutions assured the continuity of the race. In India the law of Manu (IX, 81) broke the bonds in case of sterility. Greece consigned the girl to her absolute future master; in Rome, out of the unlimited power of the father, woman went over to the domination of another man: *in manum alterius,* which explains the ancient name for this marriage of unconditional submission, *matrimonium in manu.* The Lex Poppaea had already severely penalized the unmarried and those spouses without children.

Matrimonium comes from *matris munus;* the Greek term *gamos* comes from the root *gen,* birth. The image of Plato, that of a torch of life passed along from one generation to the next, thereby assuring the future of the State and the City, is found again in Justinian and in Leo the Wise, for whom marriage assures the continuity of the human race and the immortality of the species. The words of Demosthenes that formerly rang out in open court ("We have wives to bear us children, concubines for the daily care of our persons, mistresses we keep for the sake of pleasure")[5] have lost none of their brutal candor over the centuries. The "Christian" bourgeoisie of the nineteenth century was able to make that view its own. The ancient concept associated two people for the purposes of good management of the household and of educating children, in order to assure the recruitment of citizens for the City. Certain Church Fathers assimilated this idea in their own way and justified marriage only in so far as it "brings forth virgins," populates the convents, and completes the number of saints. "If there were no married people, would there be virgins?" Methodius of Olympus asks innocently.[6] "Either we marry in order to raise children, or we live in continence for the rest of our lives," writes Justin Martyr.[7] Even for St Basil, otherwise an admirable contemplative of the mystery of the Trinity, but who speaks here as a father of the monastic rules, "Marriage is honorable if it is contracted, not in view of pleasure, but for the purpose of having children."[8] The expectation of the Messiah in the Old Testament becomes the collective messianism of the saints and justifies sexual reproduction. The ontological priesthood of the believers is reduced to a functional priesthood of recruitment.

The early Christian writers were not able to disregard the prevailing mentality. They were reacting against moral decadence; but in agreement with the ancients, they con-

---

[5]*Against Neaera* 122. Trans. A. Murray, *Private Orations* III, The Loeb Classical Library (Harvard, 1939), p. 445-46.

[6]*The Symposium: A Treatise on Chastity*, PG 18:46.

[7]*The First Apology*, chap. 29, PG 6:373; trans. Thomas B. Falls, *The Fathers of the Church*, vol. VI (Washington, 1948), p. 65.

[8]*Liber de virginitate*, chap. 38, PG 30:745. There has quite likely never existed a fiancé who would declare to a girl that he is marrying her "with an eye to pleasure," nor the one who would crudely say that he and she are cheefully going to dedicate themselves to procreation.

sidered woman, socially, as a minor and the servant (*ancilla*) of her husband, being obliged before all else to serve the husband as a master (*servire viro sicut domino*). Within this mentality, especially in the West, procreation took precedence over everything else, and man was first procreator and *pater familias*. For St Ambrose, procreation is the sole reason for marriage: *Feminis haec [prolis] sola est causa nubendi*.[9] Likewise, for St Augustine, of the threefold good of marriage —offspring (*proles*), fidelity (*fides*), sanctification (*sacramentum*)[10]—the one that predominates in the end is procreation, and he considers that precisely here woman brings her "help" to man. St Thomas says: The begetting of children is most essential in marriage (*Proles est essentialissimum in matrimonoio*). Roman Catholic Canon Law (canon 1013) faithfully expresses the thesis that has become classic: The primary end of marriage is the procreation and education of offspring (*Matrimonii finis primarius est procreatio atque educatio prolis*). Everything else is subordinated to this primary aim.

The command "be fruitful and multiply," addressed alike to the animal world and to the human being as "male and female,"[11] has caused Western theologians completely to lose sight of the fundamental fact that the institutional word of marriage, addressed to man as man-woman above the animal plane, does not even mention procreation.[12]

Two Key Concepts

It cannot be denied that the current Christian doctrine of marriage has been built on a finalistic philosophy. The under-

[9]PL 15:1632B, note 52.

[10]*The Good of Marriage*, chap. 24, PL 34:396. [The text may be read in *The Fathers of the Church*, vol. 27 (1955), p. 47ff.]

[11]Origen draws attention to this fact (see his *Commentary on Matthew*, Book XIV, chap. 16, PG 13:1229). In the Book of Genesis (1:27-28) the distinction of the sexes is a common animal function of the transmission of life. This perspective applies the term "male and female" (Gn 6:19; 7:16) to man and animals indiscriminately.

[12]It speaks of the "solitude" of the nuptial communion (Gn 2:18-24). Likewise, the teaching of the Lord (Mt 19:5; Mk 10:4), and that of St Paul (Eph 5:31).

lying influences of Hindu Buddhism, Persian dualism, Manichaeism, and Gnosticism agreed with the ancient philosophy that denied the existence of woman as a person. For Aristotle, only the masculine is "the measure of all things," man is preeminent. Woman is a defective male, a less perfect being.

A Catholic thinker, R. Flacelière, writes prudently but clearly: "The classic exposition of the aims of marriage . . . is developed especially by St Augustine; then, with greater systematization, by St Thomas Aquinas. We dare say that this theology does not strike us as expressing the essence of Christian marriage in an entirely fortunate manner. One should not forget that St Thomas was, on the one hand, dependent upon Aristotle (and notably upon his biological views), and, on the other hand, upon the Church Fathers . . . who had not been able completely to disregard the social organization of their time." And further: "If he [St Thomas] gives [love] a rather humble and subordinate place, it is on account of a mentality that came from the past and that still persisted in the thirteenth century."[13]

This heritage, according to one of the most eminent Catholic theologians, the Rector of Tübingen University, F. X. Arnold, "has led more than one Neoplatonic Father, more than one ascetic of the early Church to regrettable mistakes . . . The biological error of Aristotle (the denial of biological equality) has moreover made its way into the thought of these Christian theologians who thought themselves obliged to consider the Stagyrite as *the* Philosopher *par excellence*. Even the prince of High Scholasticism, St Thomas Aquinas, has been the victim of the harmful effects of Aristotelian thought on the question that concerns us."[14]

Indeed, one rediscovers here the germ of *the first key concept* of most of the theological treatises. "It was necessary to make woman as a partner in the work of procreation; not indeed to help in any other work, as some have maintained, because where most work is concerned man can get help more

---

[13]*Amour humain, Parole divine* (Paris, 1947), p. 18-20.

[14]*La femme dans l'Eglise* (Paris, 1955), p. 34, 37. Cf. Albert Mitterer, "L'homme et la femme dans l'Univers biologique de saint Thomas," *Zeitschrift für katholische Theologie* (Innsbruck, 1933).

conveniently from another man than from a woman."[15] For
such a biology, which is proved by today's science to be rudi-
mentary and false, the sire is man; woman is but an auxiliary
furnishing the matter. From this point there is but one more
step to say that: "by nature, woman is inferior to man,"[16]
and, save in the case of the cloistered nun, to contest her
direct relationship with God.[17] Man alone rises to God in a
direct relationship.[18]

Increasingly the idea took root that woman is entirely in
the service of nature, reduced to being merely a perpetual
womb. Such a concept allows one to say that the redemption
of woman is twofold: the one, which is universal, applies to
everyone; the second, which is specific, redeems woman from
the *original sin of her femininity*.[19]

Many ascetics would quite voluntarily claim as their own
the pessimistic view of Schopenhauer, which situates woman
between man and animal. A trap of nature, demonically
clever, she leads man to marriage and to copulation. Or the
view, so famous, of Nietzsche: in woman everything has its
solution, pregnancy. In the same manner Kant, in his *Metaphysical Elements of Justice,* formulates his famous definition
of marriage: as a contract whereby each surrenders to the
other the rights over the whole person during life, a legalized
reciprocal use of one's sexual attributes. The entire mystery
of love is reduced to the contract of a reproductive cell. The
cell is inserted into a legal and sociological context, it pro-
liferates for a while, multiplies, then, one day, it declines and
disappears, and is replaced by another.

The second key concept goes back to St Augustine, whose
influence on the thinking of theologians remains decisive even
in our days.[20] For the doctor of the theology of original sin,

[15]Thomas Aquinas, *Summa Theologiae,* 1a, quaestio 92, 1.
[16]*Ibid.,* q. 92, art. 2 ad 2.
[17]Mitterer, *op. cit.,* p. 536.
[18]See Hermann Schell, *Dogmatique* (Paderborn, 1893).
[19]See Oda Schneider, *Vom Priestertum der Frau* (Vienna, 1940).
[20]In *La Bible et l'origine de l'homme* (Desclée de Brouwer, 1961), J. de
Fraine, the well-known theologian, fortunately adds a very important rectifica-
tion. He synthetizes the doctrine of the Western Church and specifies its
dogmatic elements. On the subject of the Council of Trent he writes, "Since
the Council itself did not wish formally to establish the dogmatic character

concupiscence, which most strongly reveals that sin, is always mingled with the conjugal act; *man is embarrassed about it,* but the positive goal of procreation pardons it. The act is a means entirely determined by the end that one has in sight.[21] Ascetically speaking, marriage is a remedy against lust, *remedium concupiscentiae,* tolerated and legitimized in view of the good of procreation, *bonum prolis. Concupiscentia est malum quo quis bene utitur,* marriage is but a concession made to nature and *a state in which venial sin is inherent. De bono conjugali* establishes a decreasing hierarchy of the three goals of marriage: *bonum prolis, bonum fidei, bonum sacramenti.* Although marriage is an ecclesial institution, the perfect are called nevertheless to limit the usage of it and to direct themselves toward complete continence.

One can see that the spring itself is muddied. Before preparing a theology from initial Biblical truths, one begins with the Fall and locks everything into the physiological, and it is from the outset that marriage appears unbalanced, marked with the wound of guilt. From this negative and prohibitive aspect, an obsession with the sexual will inevitably spring forth. Love, the nuptial community, the *why* for which man has been created man-woman, constitutes this accessory remnant that more easily allows pardoning a wrong but useful action.

With St Jerome, the statement of St Paul, "but I say this as a concession,"[22] *hoc autem dico secundum indulgentiam,* is strongly advanced—above all, marriage needs indulgence and pardon. But long before him, Denis of Corinth (160) advised "not to impose the heavy burden of continence . . . but to have consideration for the *infirmity of men.*"[23] We have already seen that this "infirmity," when it is "too passionate,"

of the corporeal mode of inclusion, are we not justified in saying that the physical transmission by means of generation does not directly belong to the elements of dogma? . . . In all probability, the physical and bodily transmission of sin does not belong directly to revealed dogma." This clear precision invites theologians to be more prudent in their often gratuitous affirmations. We may also recall the encyclical *Divino afflante Spiritu,* and note that there are very few Biblical texts whose meaning has been dogmatized.

[21]PL 44:730, 460; 40:381.
[22]1 Co 7:6.
[23]PG 20:387.

turns into adultery, even under the sign of the sacrament. Concupiscence therefore constitutes the nucleus of conjugal relations, for it serves as an instrument for the transmission of original sin.[24] The sexual instinct is identified with evil desire. Such a disparagement, which is not at all in the Gospel, explains the usual prohibitions of conjugal love for almost every day of the week in the thirteenth-century West. Marital relationships entailing a kind of defilement prevented the full participation of the spouses in the liturgical life. It was especially married women who were but very rarely admitted to communion; even a woman like St Elisabeth of Thüringen received communion only at the three great feasts. In the *Waning of the Middle Ages,* Huizinga writes: "A direct line of thought links the magical fear that causes primitive people to turn away from all phenomena of feminine life, with the ascetic hatred and scorn for woman that, since Tertullian and Jerome, poison Christian literature."[25] Scholasticism goes so far as to decompose the conjugal act into both an intention that is meritorious and a physical pleasure that is virtually guilty. Sin is inherent to it: concupiscence infects the seed of life. One notices a misleading schematization as well as scholarly analyses that distort life and discourage even yearning after sainthood. The current teaching

[24]This is only a theological opinion, a *theologoumenon.* By contrast, Ignatius of Antioch, while speaking of the need for the approval of the bishop, specifies, "in order that their marriage may be in accordance with the Lord's will and not to gratify desire" (*To Polycarp,* 5. 2; trans. E. J. Goodspeed, *The Apostolic Fathers,* New York, 1950, p. 234). The grace of the sacrament transforms, and the nature of the passion is changed. Thus Clement of Alexandria says, "I hold that even the seed of the sanctified is holy" (*Stromateis* III. 6, trans. J. E. L. Oulton, in *Alexandrian Christianity,* Philadelphia, 1954, p. 62); "Sin, the corruptible, cannot be in communion with the incorruptible," and the incorruptible, *aphtharsia,* points to the Eucharist (*Strom.* III. 10). St Gregory of Nazianzus writes, "Art thou not yet wedded to flesh? Fear not this consecration: thou art pure even after marriage" (*Oration* 40. 18, *On Holy Baptism,* trans. Charles B. Browne, *A Select Library of Nicene and Post-Nicene Fathers,* series 2, vol. VII, New York, 1894, p. 365). It would be useless to continue. The quotations are numerous, and they all state the same truth about the holiness of marriage. By contrast, the concept of marriage as a remedy against concupiscence leads Abelard to state that it is not a sacrament like the others, because it does not cause grace (PL 178:1745)!
[25]As quoted by F. X. Arnold, *op. cit.,* p. 141, note 57.

of moral theology today burdens the conscience with a guilt complex, and even today conditions the innumerable conflicts of married life that are relegated to psychiatry and to the morbid.

Anthropological pessimism, as it came down from St Augustine, caused Luther to say that marriage, of course, is better than "papist virginity"; however, marriage remains sullied from the evil of concupiscence that affects all terrestrial things. Finality shows marriage ordained for the good of the earthly city, and it is up to the State to take care of it, since it is a "natural" institution.[26] Even if Calvin found more noble terms to speak of the holiness of conjugal life, marriage is nonetheless only an "honorable estate," not a sacrament, and remains likewise a social and earthly institution. From the Protestant point of view, the religious ceremony adds nothing to marriage, but is necessary for the integration of the couple into the congregation of the faithful. The tendency is to depart from a current idea, that of a "nuptial benediction."[27] The Reformed Churches do not counsel continence. Although the vocation to the celibate life is scriptural, it is only a strictly personal call; there can exist neither an imposed rule nor a spiritual method of the monastic type.[28] No suspicion of the sexual life is noted, but there is great distrust toward all theories of "sublimation," out of fear of hidden harmonics between the mystical and the sexual. Every mystical ascension—Eros—is taken to signal a violation of the frontier between the Creator and the creature. There is only Agape, the descending path of God toward man, that abolishes Eros and its sublimation and restricts purity, which is circumscribed within strictly moral borders.

Within Christendom, the anti-Christian tendency to scorn the value of virginity reinforces, by reaction, the distance be-

[26]See Baranovski, *Luthers Lehre von der Ehe* (1913).

[27]J. Ellul, "Position des Eglises protestantes à l'égard de la famille," in *Renouveau des idées sur la famille,* Cahier n. 18 (Paris, 1954). On the other hand, one can point out a current reaction in favor of the sacramentality of marriage: see H. Leenhardt, *Le Mariage chrétien* (1946). See also Calvin, *Textes choisis,* eds. Ch. Gagnebien and Karl Barth (1948), pp. 206-11; Max Thurian, *Mariage et Célibat* (1955).

[28]A strong and fortunate reaction is shown by the very existence of Protestant monastic communities.

tween a heroic celibacy of the elect and the average life of weak and defective souls. The prevailing pastoral theology, in catechisms and theological treatises, is amazingly poor.[29] The believer, a member of the royal priesthood who is called to total consecration in the form of a nuptial ministry, is given the place of an adolescent minor, inept in every way, who is from the outset instilled with a feeling of inferiority and guilt. This view overlooks a fundamental psychological fact: at the moment of love's inception, all carnal thought is totally absent, completely excluded. St John Chrysostom understood it well, saying that the only effective remedy for depravity and concupiscence is the *magnus amor*. But the average ascetic, consumed as he is with a secret and incessant temptation, can never look favorably upon the dispensation and free enjoyment of what appears to him to be the one attraction of married life. We are no longer speaking the same language; it seems that we are in the presence of two worlds that no longer understand each other.

The Myths

In a world that is essentially masculine—where everything is placed under the sign of the Patriarchate—man, armed with his reason, rationalizes being and existence, loses his cosmic attachment to the sky, to nature, and also to woman as the mystery that completes his own being. Eliminating everything irrational that disturbs him and sliding toward abstractions, man sees the dimension of profundity closed. He lays out the great avenues of civilization, clear, spacious, and regular, where the place of woman, prepared in advance, is that of a minor. From an instinctive self-defense, man

[29]See the study by S. de Lestapis, "Evolution de la pensée exprimée de l'Eglise catholique," in *Renouveau des idées sur la famille*, a work published under the direction of R. Prigent (Paris, 1954). While commenting on the nineteenth century, he writes, "Only Mgr. Dupanloup represents the exception. Indeed, he believes that the spouses are also called to holiness, something that no one had dared to assert in his time . . . He has the courage to speak of nuptial love and to propose the latter as the great means of perfection for the spouses, and this occurred in 1884!" (p. 260, 261).

enslaves woman, as if she were an evil force, a permanent threat to his freedom. In appearance man will give woman all the honors, but he will situate her where she will never more be able to harm him. There she is subject to the supreme power of the chief, to the indisputable authority of man, her master and lord. Man possesses her as he does his land, all the more so since woman symbolizes the earth, the chthonic element, if not also the lunar, deceptive aspect. Man is the sun principle, clarity. He transforms into curses the physiology of woman, even her femininity, her gifts, and her charisms.

In the laws of Manu or of Solon, in Leviticus, in the Roman Code or the Koran, everywhere woman is considered as an inferior being without rights. The Pythagorean maxim states: "the principle of good creates order, light, man; the principle of evil creates chaos, darkness, woman." For Aristotle, matter is female and movement is male, which means that woman belongs to another dimension; she does not entirely belong to the human community. "Woman is female by virtue of a certain lack of quality." She is "other"; but, according to Plato, otherness is negation, evil, and this is why he thanks the gods that he is a man. In order to avenge man, the gods invent woman; it is Pandora who lets loose all the evils. And so with woman passivity, multiplicty, matter, and disorder take root in life.

The Greek woman was confined to the gyneceum; her ideal was Penelope. In *Politica,* Aristotle declares: "Silence is a woman's glory." The woman in Rome is handed over as a "thing" (*res*) to fulfill the needs of man. Jewish, or simply masculine, antifeminism starts from the simplistic idea that woman is taken from man's side, and it is on this side that men have come to ruin innumerable times. The ritual demanded a purification of the mother that was twice as long after the birth of a daughter. Among the Eighteen Benedictions one hears: "Blessed art thou, O Lord our God, who hast not made me a woman." Even St Paul appears to bow to this tradition when he speaks of the total submission of the woman. And Ecclesiastes states: "One man in a thousand I may find, but never a woman better than the rest." The

Gospel (Jn 4:27) shows the disciples surprised by the simple fact that Christ speaks to a woman.

St Augustine expresses a current conception when he reports that the married woman is legally incompetent. When speaking of Monica, Augustine observes in his *Confessions* that the woman should above all serve her man the master and be her husband's handmaid (*ancilla*).[30] For St Thomas, women must keep silent because the "weakness of their reason" renders them incapable of teaching, of presiding, or of exercising the office of lawyer![31] Most often, Scholastic exegesis comments on the Biblical narrative of the Creation in the same sense: woman has been created *for* man as his servant, help, object. Nietzsche draws logical inferences from this: "Woman is the diversion of the warrior." In like manner, Kierkegaard's flight from the woman is justified metaphysically: "It is a woman's misfortune to represent everything in the moment and to represent nothing more in the next moment, without ever comprehending her own meaning as woman." The idealized and poeticized being rises in the sky like a brilliant star; she is the illumination of the feast, but afterward she vanishes and falls into the abyss. In *Physiology of Marriage,* Balzac synthesizes the wisdom of a thousand years: "Woman is a slave that one must know how to place on a throne." "Woman, the relative being," says Michelet; dream of man, she is but a poetic form of absence; this is why, according to Julien Benda, "man can be thought of without woman, she can never be thought of without man." Therein lies the entire difference.

The conflict is irreducible. Man seeks to assert himself by overstepping that which confines him. But every woman is a boundary. Many may desire the restorative sleep beside the maternal spring; he may be passionately attracted to the opposite pole of his being, but he will always resent this adventure as soon as it is prolonged, as demeaning his virility, a prison that restricts his horizons and confines his spirit. Such is history.

[30]See R. Laprat, "Le rôle de la mater familias romaine d'après saint Augustin," in *Revue du Moyen Age latin* (I, 1945).
[31]*Commentary on I Cor 14:34.*

As an oyster secretes its shell, the *superego* of the collective consciousness secretes untruthful myths. It is to women that the ritual prescriptions defined during the Rabbinic era still apply today. Facing Christ, in whom "there is neither male nor female," are humans stigmatized by ancient maledictions.[32] Even the Book of Revelation contains traces of the Judaeo-Christian mentality and emphasizes the woman who defiles man (Rv 14:4). The weakness of man retaliates, exactly as in the symptomatic Biblical narrative of Susanna and the elders. An analysis of the myths created by deceitful historical configurations would easily point out the sterility of this transfer of blame to the woman. This is the "Adam complex," a thoroughly masculine one: "It was the woman who gave me the fruit of the tree."

Man has desecrated love, even before discovering its nature. Nowhere else are there so many lies and such hypocrisy, precisely because love is the deepest thirst for the truth, the very voice of a being. The mass, the crowd, swarms more and more in the erotic pit, the rounds of which made so quickly, ending in "nausea." St John Chrysostom raises a violent protest: "The gift of God, the root of our generation is insulted. This then let us cleanse away with our discourse. I am desirous of having marriage purified, so as to bring it back again to its proper nobleness, so as to stop the mouth of the heretics . . ."[33]

The Charisms Of Woman

Woman has her mode of being, her own form of existence, the gift of weaving her entire being through her special relationship to God, others, and self. In the course of history, the social environment fashions or distorts the types of the feminine. Nevertheless, woman safeguards at the very depth of her self the mystery of her being and of her charisms that

---

[32]See Peter Browe, S. J., *Beiträge zur Sexualethik des Mittelalters* (Breslau, 1932).

[33]*Homily XII on Colossians*. Trans. *Nicene and Post-Nicene Fathers*, series 1, vol. XIII (Grand Rapids, Rept. 1979), p. 319.

St Paul designates with the symbol of the "veil" (1 Co 11).
It is this mystery that she must "unveil" and interpret in order
to understand her destiny "nuptially," in close relationship
with that of man. The Biblical account of the creation of Eve
(which is more truly a birth because Eve is separated or proceeds from Adam) is correctly set up as the original archetype of the consubstantiality of *complementary* principles.
The masculine and feminine form the archetypal human
monad: Adam-Eve. The Fall breaks up this oneness into a bad
masculinity and a bad femininity: couples made of two polar-
ized, objectified, and separate individuals, situated outside
each other, placed nonetheless side by side. From this comes
the distance itself between the two poles of human existence:
either they are opposites marred by discord and a fruitless
contention, or they are unlikes who accept one another, com-
plementaries who love each other, the conjunction of opposites. The second solution presupposes the grace that recapitulates the initial cell in Christ and is placed at the heart of
marriage, the "sacrament of love," according to St John
Chrysostom's admirable formulation. The nuptial community
arises as the prophetic figure of the Kingdom of God: the
ultimate unity, the community of the Masculine and the
Feminine in their totality in God.

The Mother

*And the man called his wife's
name* Hawwah, *that is, "Life," because she was the mother of all
living.*

The Biblical term *Ezer Ke-negdo* (Gn 2:18) means "a helper
turned toward him" (the man). Looked at more inwardly,
this means that woman is completely at ease within the limits
of her being and develops it into a clear, limpid symphony.
She fills the world with her being, with her radiant presence.
Man, on the other hand, overreaches his being; more outside
himself, his charism of expansion makes him look outward.

He fills the world with his creative energies by asserting himself as master and lord. He accepts at his side the woman, his help. She is at once his betrothed, his wife, and his mother. "The glory of man," according to St Paul (1 Co 11:7), in her luminous purity, she is like a mirror that reflects the face of man, reveals man to himself and thereby betters him. Thus she helps man understand himself and realize the meaning of his own existence. She accomplishes this by deciphering his destiny, for it is through woman that man more easily becomes what he is.

This is the entire dialectic of spiritual motherhood. The words of St Peter (1 Pt 3:4) are addressed to every woman and contain an entire gospel of the feminine; they define her essential charism accurately: to give birth to the hidden man of the heart—*homo cordis absconditus.* Man is more inclined to be interested in only his own cause; on the other hand, the maternal instinct of the woman, as at the wedding of Cana (Jn 2:1-10), immediately discovers the thirst of the spirit of men and finds the eucharistic spring to quench it. The relation so mysterious between mother and child causes woman—Eve, the source of life—to watch over every being, to protect life and the world.

The question of knowing whether the woman will be wife, mother, or bride of Christ (*sponsa Christi*) is only secondary. Her charism of interiorized and universal "maternity" carries every woman toward the hungry and the needy and admirably defines the feminine essence: virgin or spouse, every woman is a mother for all eternity (*in aeternum*). The structure of her soul predisposes her "to protect" all that crosses her path, to discover in the strongest and most virile being a weak, defenseless child.

If man is forever inclined to poeticize woman, if he remains an incurable romantic, woman is the only one to love man for what he is and as he is. A woman's love is the most profound enigma, and man will never cease to be amazed at it. Helvetius defines masculine love very well: "to love is to need." For which the feminine formula would be: "to love is to fulfill the need," to go beyond and even to anticipate it. Save for the deviations of "narcissism," or those of the "virago" or of the "Diana complex," the maternal spirit colors all forms of a woman's affectivity. The renunciation that life always imposes is shown as the great purification of all the purely biological desire for possession. Out of being unconscious it can be elevated to the grandeur of the sorrowing mother (*mater dolorosa*) of the judgment of Solomon, or to the very sword that pierces the soul of the Virgin Mary.

"Jesus seeing His mother and the disciple He loved standing near her, said to His mother, 'Woman, this is your son.'" Herein lies a fundamental utterance about woman; one senses that it transcends all biological motherhood. The archetype of the Great Mother (*Magna Mater*) determines all forms of the feminine; it lies at the depth of every woman's soul; the eternal virgin, the eternal feminine, derives from the "eternal motherly," the only true one, because it is universal and full of the Pleroma.

Woman: Spiritual Instrument of Human Nature

The theology of the Church Fathers centers on the philanthropy[34] of the Father. We confess the same: "I believe in God [who is before all] the Father almighty"; the Spirit forms in us the Name of God: "Abba Father," and the divine Sonship is placed at the center of Pauline theology. The "fatherhood" of God determines His fundamental relationship with man, His son.

Man is created in the image of God, but in reality, a man does not possess the paternal instinct in the same way as a woman possesses the maternal instinct. Man (masculine) has nothing immediate *in his nature* that would spontaneously reproduce the religious category of paternity. But, an ancient liturgical text of dogmatic content (the *Theotokion*) defines the motherhood of the Virgin in the light of the paternity of God: "Without a father have you given birth to the Son, the One who was born without a mother before all ages." The analogy is clearly described: *the maternity of the Virgin presents itself as the human figure of the paternity of God*. If

---

[34]A liturgical expression signifying God's benevolence toward mankind.

fatherhood is the category of divine life, *motherhood* is the religious category of the human life.

Conqueror, adventurer, designer, man is not paternal in his essence. This truth has a far-reaching implication: it explains why the religious principle of dependence, of receptivity, of communion, is expressed more directly through woman; the special sensitivity for the truly spiritual is greater in *anima* ("the feminine") than it is in *animus* ("the masculine"); it is the feminine soul that is the least removed from the source, creation. *The Bible exalts woman as the instrument of spiritual receptivity in human nature.* Indeed, the promise of salvation has been given to woman: it is she who receives the Annunciation, it is she to whom the Resurrected Christ first appears, it is the woman adorned with the sun who represents the Church and the Heavenly City in Revelation. Likewise, it is the image of the Bride and of the Betrothed that God has chosen above all others to express His love toward man and the nuptial nature of His communion. And what is ultimately most decisive, the Incarnation is accomplished in the feminine being of the Virgin who gives to it her flesh and blood.

To the divine fatherhood as qualifying the being of God corresponds directly the motherhood of woman as the distinctive religious quality of human nature, its capacity to receive the divine. The aim of the Christian life is to make of every human being a mother, predestined for the mystery of birth, "in order that Christ be formed in you." Sanctification is the action of the Spirit who brings about the miraculous birth of Christ in the depth of the soul. The Nativity, then, expresses the charism of every woman to give birth to God in ruined souls. "The word is ever born anew in the hearts of the saints" (*The Epistle to Diognetus*). According to Maximus the Confessor, the mystic is the one in whom the birth of the Lord is manifested. And how telling it is that St Paul uses the image of motherhood when he wishes to express his spiritual fatherhood: "I must go through all the pain of childbirth."

One aspect of monastic spirituality strongly underlines

this. If in certain areas woman is not as strong as man, on the charismatic level she is, to the contrary, his perfect equal. Clement of Alexandria says: "The virtue of man and of woman is one and the same virtue . . . their conduct is of the same nature."[35] Theodoret of Cyrus commemorates women "whose struggles were not less, but greater than those of men. They are worthy of greater praise: being of a weaker nature they have shown the same courage as men and have freed their race from the ancestral dishonor."[36] Their first charism is "divine charity" and a special grace for abandoning themselves to the love of Christ. Here no one views them as spiritually inferior. They are deemed capable of giving spiritual direction to the religious on the same terms as men. A charismatic woman, illumined by God (*Theophotistos*), receives the title of spiritual mother (*ammas*).[37] Most often they are the mothers of their monastery, just as Pacomius was the father of his. People from the outside would come to seek advice from them (St Euphrasia and St Irene).

In about 1200, Abba Isaiah composed a book of sayings of the Mothers, titled *Materikon*, that was similar to a *Paterikon*. Except for the power to administer the sacraments and to teach in the Church (reserved for the episcopate), the Mothers had the same prerogatives and duties as the Fathers had with the monks. They were not Church Mothers (which elevation was reserved for the Fathers-Bishops), but they certainly were spiritual Mothers who took part in the propagation of doctrine; liturgical texts praise those who showed themselves "equal to the Apostles" (St Helena and St Nino).[38] *The Symposium* by Methodius of Olympus proves this; the *Life of Syncletica* is analogous to the *Life of Antony;* and the apophthegms of the Mothers are found in alphabetical order

[35]*Paedogogus,* Book I, PG 8:260C.
[36]Theodoret of Cyrus, *Religiosa historia,* PG 82:1489B; *Oratio de divina et sancta charitate,* PG 82:1497B; 1504AB.
[37]*Vitae Patrum,* V. 18, 19.
[38]Women have never held the priestly functions properly speaking, but they participate in evangelization and they assist the priest in what concerns women. The *Apostolic Church Order* speaks of the ordination of deaconesses through the imposition of hands, which indicates a major order; likewise, Canon XIX of the Council of Nicaea and Canon XV of the Council of Chalcedon.

among the sayings of the Fathers. St Pacomius sent the Rule of his monastery to his sister so that the sisters might be educated "according to the same guidelines." Likewise, Basil's *Rules* presuppose that the virtues of the monks will not be wanting in the nature of women.[39]

While speaking of the priesthood, the *Didascalia* specifies the mutual relationship of the two natures: "The Deacon holds the place of Christ, and you shall love him. You shall honor the Deaconesses who hold the place of the Holy Spirit." The statement is clear: in his spiritual being, man is ontologically joined to Christ; the woman is ontologically linked to the Holy Spirit. This is why in the symbolics of the liturgical assembly women are called the "altar" and represent prayer. Woman is the Orant, the image of the soul in adoration, the human being become prayer. On the well-known fresco from the catacomb of St Callistus, the man extends his hand above the bread of the offering, and he is the sacrificer, the bishop, the one who acts and celebrates. Behind him stands the Orant, the human having become religious, prayer in her very being, the pure offering and the total gift. Woman, through her prayer-being, covers life with her maternal protection; she takes life in her hands and lifts it toward God. She is under the sign of the Spirit who "hovers" (*merahefath*, the Hebrew term from the Creation story), the sign of the Paraclete: Advocate and Comforter.

Woman: Point of Encounter
Between God and Man

If the masculine takes part in the Incarnation by means of silence in the person of St Joseph ("The Word, the adopted son of silence," as Claudel calls him), it is woman, on the other hand, who pronounces the fiat, the "let it be done," on behalf of all. To the creative fiat of the Father responds the humble fiat of the "handmaid of God." This fiat is the indispensable human foundation of the Incarnation, the free

[39]*Sermo de renunciatione saeculi*, PG 31:624D, 625A. The names of Olympias, Sabiana, and Macrina come to mind.

Yes of humanity pronounced by Mary: yes, I desire my salvation, I thirst for my Savior. Christ could not take human flesh and blood if humanity—Mary—had not offered them freely as a gift, a pure offering. On Christmas Eve, the Church sings: "What shall we give Thee, O Christ? . . . Each of the creatures brings You a gift of gratitude: the angels their song; the heavens the star; the wise men their gifts; the shepherds their admiration; the earth the stable; the desert the manger; but we human beings give You a Virgin Mother." This is why, in Orthodox piety, it is the Theotokos (Mother of God) holding in her arms the Infant Jesus (and not, for example, Simeon) who is precisely the icon of the Incarnation, of the highest degree of communion between God and man, the meeting point of the two fiats.

The man Jesus knew no human father, but He knows His mother; His relation is son-mother, His bond with humanity is through maternity. The Eastern Church cherishes the word of the Lord to John, "This is your mother," and sees in it the completion of Eve; Mary is "Mother of the living," a figure of the Church in her fundamental truth of motherly protection. Orant, she is the prayer of the Church; on the icons consecrated to this theme, she is spreading the *omophorion*[40] over the world in order to "protect" it, and in eschatological compositions of the "Deisis,"[41] she appears as the one who intercedes.

As the New Eve in Christ, Mary brings us the truth about human nature; the Church declares her eternally *virgin*, virgin in her essence and *thereby mother*. It is because virginity, in its norm, blossoms into motherhood that every woman is called to the maternal.

In Greek, "chastity" (*sophrosyne*) means integrity and integration, the very power to bring together. An ancient liturgical prayer asks the "most pure Theotokos," "by your love, bind my soul" that from the aggregate of my states of

---

[40]The *omophorion* is a large strip of white wool decorated with a cross and carried by the Orthodox bishop around the neck, over the dalmatic. It symbolizes the lost sheep that Our Savior carries back to the sheep fold on His shoulders. It corresponds to the ancient Roman *pallium* of the Middle Ages.

[41]*Deisis* means supplication, intercession.

soul a single soul may spring. Only such integration is able to stop the enterprise of demolition to which modern masculine genius is dedicated. By her chaste structure, woman is called to this integration. The salvation of civilization depends upon the "eternal motherly." One understands its saving power if one realizes that it is not as "the weaker sex" that Eve has been tempted. On the contrary, she has been seduced because it is she who represents the principle of religious integrity in human nature: wounded in her heart, she immediately succumbs. Adam meekly follows her: "The woman gave me this fruit."

Left to himself, man loses his way in the labyrinth of his abstractions, in the perfected techniques of debasement. Degraded, he becomes degrading, and creates a world that responds to his dehumanized assumptions: man is in the agony of death. Insanity is the disorder of one alone, masculine reason is the collective insanity of all. The true feminine is well described by Paul Claudel, when he makes Grace say: "I am not accessible to reason, you will *not* make, you will not make of me what you please, but I sing and I dance."[42]

Man extends himself in the world by means of tools; woman accomplishes this by the gift of self. In her very being, she is linked to the rhythms of nature. But according to the norm, the physiological and psychological depend on the spirit, they serve and reveal it. Woman's physiological ability to give birth comes from her *maternal spirit*. Likewise, man is physically more virile because there is something in his spirit that corresponds to the "violence" of which the Gospel speaks: "these are the violent who lay hold of the Kingdom of God."

If the nature of man is *to act*, that of woman is *to be*—and this is the preeminent religious state. Man creates science, philosophy, art, but he distorts everything by a frightening objectification of the organized truth. Woman is contrary to all objectification because she stands in the perspective not of creation but of giving birth; she herself, by her being, is the criterion that rectifies every abstraction and recenters the

---

[42]*Cinq Grandes Odes IV,* "La Muse qui est la Grâce," *Oeuvre poétique* (Paris: Gallimard, 1957), p. 268.

values, in order correctly to manifest the masculine logos. Instinctively, woman will always uphold the primacy of being over theory, of the active over the speculative, of the intuitive over the discursive. She possesses the gift of directly "seeing" into another's life, the innate ability to grasp the imponderable, to decipher destiny. To protect the world of men as mother and to purify it as virgin, by giving to this world a soul, her soul, such is the vocation of every woman, religious, celibate, or spouse.

United to Christ the Priest, man penetrates into the elements of this world sacramentally; he consecrates and transforms the world into the Kingdom. Violent, he takes hold of the Kingdom. However, this treasure is made up of every manifestation of the sacred, of holiness of being, and it is woman who represents this. The woman wounds the dragon at the head, not through her activity, but through her very being, her purity. For the demons, it is this holiness of being that is mortally unbearable.

Outward-turning man exists in the extension of himself and in the outside projection of his spirit that dominates the world; inward-turning woman is directed toward being. The feminine operates on the level of an ontological structure: it is not a verb, it is being (esse), the creature's womb. The Theotokos gives her entire being where the Logos comes to take His place; she carries Him and she reveals Him. The liturgy identifies the Virgin with the domain of the Wisdom of God and glorifies in her the accomplished aim of God's creation: termino fisso d'eterno consiglio (of the eternal design the Cornerstone).[43]

In Heraclitus, "war is the father of all"; by contrast, "reconciliation, concord, is the mother of all."[44] He gives the amazing image of the bow and the lyre. In Greek, it is the same word "bios" that designates the bow and life, that which kills and that which brings to life. The father—war— is symbolized by the bow, and the mother—harmony—by the

[43]Dante Alighieri, Paradiso, Canto XXXIII, v. 3; trans. Laurence Binyon, The Divine Comedy (New York, 1947), p. 539.

[44]Heraclitus: The Cosmic Fragments, ed. C. S. Kirk (Cambridge, 1962), p. 245, 201.

lyre. We may say that the lyre is a noble bow, one with several strings; instead of death it sings of life. In this manner the warlike, the murderous, the masculine may be *attuned,* made noble by the feminine, and changed into life, culture, cult, and eschatological liturgy. The sacrament of marriage unites charisms that are complementary and is the prerequisite for a special form of the priesthood of all believers.

The Personalistic Conception of Marriage

Social life requires married people just as it requires farmers and soldiers. Its utilitarianism can even justify the polygamy of the Old Testament or of the Code of Hammurabi (paragraph 145) that legalized fertile concubines and ranked them equal to wives. Here the good of the species comes before that of the individuals. Society is only interested in the biological and sociological content of nuptial unions. It does not have to arrive at a conclusion about love, and when it speaks of love, it implies the family and not love.

Love flees these forms and even escapes from the religious, when the latter does not address itself adequately to the mystery of love. Such a "sentimental education" produces divisions, secularizes, and in the end separates from the Church. On the other hand, current teaching hardly encourages nuptial spiritualization in itself; socialized, it merely sets forth banalities on procreative love. Yet, the doctrine of the Scholastics is not the only one and can in no way pretend to be the Tradition. It is appropriate to recall the words of St Benedict in his Rule: "There are ways which to men seem right, but the ends thereof lead to the depths of hell" (Pr 16:25).[45]

The seeds deposited in the Bible flower only after many centuries. A completely new spirituality is asserting itself today, one that is searching for neither more nor less than a priestly vocation in conjugal love: *The Nuptial Priesthood.*

---

[45]*The Rule of Saint Benedict,* trans. Oswald H. Blair, in *The Way to God* by Emmanuel Heufelder (Kalamazoo: Cistercian Publications, 1983), p. 237.

It is only by rising above the philosophy of the "common good" that one can grasp the singular worth of those who love each other. It is this hidden and intimate element that is consecrated in the sacrament, it is love that constitutes its matter and receives the gift of the Holy Spirit, the nuptial Pentecost. Society knows but the surface. Between the two lovers there is only God who is the third term; this is why the meaning of marriage is taken precisely in this dual and direct relation to God.

In ancient Greek mysteries and rituals, marriage was called the *telos*, "end," in the sense of conclusion, plenitude. Pseudo-Dionysius the Areopagite explains this: "The Athenians called marriage '*telos*,' because it crowns a man for life."[46] Likewise, in Plato, *Eros* is the longing for completion.

V. Soloviev, in *The Meaning of Love*, which is perhaps the most perceptive of his writings, reconnects love not to the species, but to the person. Procreation fragments the person, love makes him whole. Soloviev shows that in lower organisms, there is at once great reproductive power and a complete absence of sexual attraction, from the very fact that the sexes are not differentiated. With more advanced organisms, the sexual attraction increases as the reproductive force diminishes, until, at the summit, with man, the strongest sexual love becomes visible, even in the case of a total absence of reproduction. And thus, if at the two extremes of animal life we find, on the one hand, reproduction without sexual love, and, on the other, sexual love without reproduction, it is apparent that these two phenomena are not indissolubly linked, that each one has its own significance and that reproduction does not emerge as the essential aim of the sexual life in its higher forms. In man the sexual differentiation finds its meaning independent of the species, of society, and of the common good. Indeed, between sexuality and procreation there is a direct physical link; it conditions the sexual attraction that is most often instinctive, impersonal, and common to to the entire animal kingdom. This power of the species over the individual reduces the persons to a simple, specific function, compatible with innumerable substitutions. On this

46PG 3:1184.

level, sexual life visibly bears the mark of man's Fall. Both the preservation of the species and selfish sexual pleasure reduce the partner to a mere tool and destroy his dignity. Love alone bestows a spiritual meaning upon marriage, and justifies it by elevating it to perceive the countenance of the beloved in God, to the level of the one and only icon.

The Church, by instituting monasticism, unerringly professes the absolute value of the individual above the social, and affirms it once again by consecrating the unique being of the lovers, by placing this ordination at the heart of the sacrament of marriage. Married love proceeds from spiritual interiority and gazes toward the inside. Its visible aspect is but an outer manifestation. Its invisible aspect is open only to faith, because faith is precisely the perception of things not seen. "It is in the vision of the beloved that love grows," Theodoret says;[47] "the one who loves has another self," St John Chrysostom states.[48]

Without multiplying quotations, one can detect an entire tradition that matured in the shadow of a certain kenosis[49] of love. Origen emphasizes that it is God who joins together the two in one.[50] St John Chrysostom sees in every marriage the image of the wedding at Cana, and thus the real presence of Christ.[51] The "Lord comes there always to perform the same miracle," according to St Cyril of Alexandria.[52] "Christ has been invited in order to encompass marriage with chastity . . . and to fill future afflictions with grace," St Epiphanius declares.[53] In his *Moral Poems*, St Gregory of Nazianzus teaches that all human culture originates in the nuptial communion, "but in it there is something still higher and better.

[47]*De sancto Amore.*

[48]PG 51:30; *Homily II on Thessalonians,* PG 62:406.

[49]*Kenosis*: self-emptying, humbling, the veil of humility hiding the Divinity of the Word in His Incarnation (cf Ph 2:7).

[50]Origen, *Commentary on Matthew,* Book XIV, PG 13:1230.

[51]*In illud, propter fornicationes uxorem,* PG 51:210.

[52]*In Joannis Evangelium* Liber II, PG 73:224.

[53]*Adversus haereses* Liber II, tomus I, PG 41:942. One is far removed from the idea of "pleasure" as well as from all excessive concern with procreation. What is crucial is the integrity of the spirit, its fullness.

. . . Marriage is the key that opens the door to chastity and perfect love."[54]

One may also mention the Franciscan tradition of St Bonaventure in the West, of Richard of Middleton, or of Duns Scotus.[55] Here the finalistic doctrine of the Scholastics no longer applies; the primary aim is the good of the sacrament (*bonum sacramenti*). The *sacramentum* is matrimony properly speaking; fidelity (*fides*) and procreation (*proles*) belong to the conjugal ministry (*officium conjugii*). For Hugh of St-Victor, the root of marriage lies in the bond of charity, in the union of hearts.[56] "Conjugal love is the sacrament of realized communion between Christ and the Church by the effect of the Incarnation."[57] At the end of the Middle Ages certain preachers (in reaction to the Albigenses) raised the value of marriage even to placing it before the religious profession. Married people were considered as forming an order. According to Robert de Sorbon it is a holy order (*sacer ordo*); for the Dominican Peregrinus, the order of spouses has God as its abbot.

Thus in the East as in the West one notes an unbroken tradition. In full agreement with Biblical teaching it strongly supports the personal meaning by showing the lovers being one for the other, one toward the other. Conjugal life does not have to be "pardoned," it is a value in itself. The East, always faithful to the personalistic conception, can only rejoice at seeing in the West a team of modern theologians whose thought is applied to the same personalistic aspect of marriage. The following may be cited: *Le sens et but du mariage*, by Herbert Doms (1935); the Dutch Hoegen; *Die zweckfrage der Ehe in neuer Beleuchtung*, by the Swiss Bernadin Krempel (1945); N. Rocholl's *Die Ehe als geweihtes Leben* (1936). These works establish love as the primary reason for the existence of marriage. Beside the classical concept, it is also this meaning that one finds set forth in the

---

[54]*Poemata moralia*, sectio II, PG 37:541-542.

[55]See Binkowski, "Die Ehegüter nach Duns Scot," in *Wissenschaft und Weisheit* (1940).

[56]See Cl. Schahl, *La doctrine des fins du mariage dans la théologie scolastique* (1946).

Encyclical Letter of Pius XI, *On Christian Marriage* (1930):
"[love] must have as its primary purpose that man and wife
help each other in forming and perfecting themselves in the
interior life, so that through their partnership in life they may
advance ever more and more in virtue; . . . this mutual inward
molding of husband and wife . . . can in a very real sense . . .
be said to be the chief reason and purpose of matrimony."[58]

Man and woman move toward one another by "mutually
getting to know each other," by revealing themselves to each
other for a shared ascent; nothing comes to ennoble or legiti-
mize, still less to "pardon" this meaning that royally imposes
itself before, or even independent of, procreation.

It is from this overflowing fullness that the child can
come as fruit, but it is not procreation that determines and
establishes the value of marriage. St John Chrysostom says:
"When there is no child, will they not be two? Most certainly, for their coming together has this effect, it diffuses and
commingles the bodies of both. And as one who has cast
ointment into oil, who has made the whole one, so in truth it
is also here."[59] "Two souls so united have nothing to fear.
With harmony, peace and mutual love, man and woman own
all possessions. They can live in peace behind the impregnable
wall that protects them, which is love according to God. By
love's grace, they are harder than diamond and stronger than
iron, they sail in abundance, steer a course toward eternal
glory and attract more and more grace from God."[60] "Marriage
is the intimate union of two lives,"[61] "the sacrament of
love."[62]

[57]*Hugonis de Sancto Victore Opuscula* Pars II: dogmatica, PL 176:860.
[58]*Seven Great Encyclicals,* ed. William J. Gibbon, S. J. (New York:
Paulist Press, 1963), p. 84. By contrast, the Decree of the Holy Office of
March 29, 1944, reverts to the old concept and subordinates the communion
of love to the service of procreation. It does not dispute the community of
love but makes it instrumental to the interest of the species and of the common good. See R. Boigelot, "Du sens de la fin du mariage," in *Nouvelle
Revue théologique* (1939), p. 5-33; and E. Boissard, *Question théologique
sur le mariage* (1948).
[59]*Homily XII on Colossians,* 5-6; trans. *Nicene and Post-Nicene Fathers,*
series 1, vol. XIII (Rept. 1979), p. 319.
[60]*Homily XXXVIII on Genesis* 7.
[61]*Peri gamou, On Marriage* III. 3.
[62]*Homily III on I Corinthians, Quales ducendae sint uxores,* PG 51:230.

The Ultimate Light

Love does not depend on the "order of the day," but on the order of the last day. The agraphon quoted by Clement of Rome clearly indicates this. To Salome's question, "When will the Kingdom of God come?" the Lord said, "When you will destroy the vestment of shame, when the two shall be one, and the male with the female neither male nor female . . ."[63]

All the contradictions of human nature are manifested in sexual life, for it is there that human nature is most vulnerable and carries a deep wound. When the sexual attraction is impersonal, it is the source of the most odious profanations and of the most humiliating enslavement of the human spirit. It is not the unique, but the anatomy and the moment and the "brief eternity of pleasure" that are sought and desired. Freed from sexual taboos, perfected techniques sharpen the perverted senses of eroticism and descend below the animal, and man drinks his shame and his sickness.

Outside Eden, the physiological by itself debases. According to Jacob Boehme, the virgin flew away and the earth knows only bad masculinity and bad femininity clothed with the "vestment of shame," which instinctive sexual modesty indicates. But with the coming of the Theotokos, the virgin is once again among men and chastity seeks its hour to offer itself as the purifying leaven of the human being. When the angel of Revelation declares that "there will be no more time," he announces likewise the destruction of the "vestment of shame" and the virginal restoration of the human spirit: "when two will be one," the Masculine and the Feminine of the Kingdom, Adam-Eve reconstituted as one single virginal Being.

In history, if one is not among the saints, marriage is but a sociological cell, the legalized mating of those who "know not what they do." The entire dignity of marriage, according to the agraphon quoted, is revealed only at the appointed time, for it demands a great maturity of spirit and ascetic mastery of the Last Days. The alpha always carries its omega:

[63]This agraphon is found in chapter 12 of II Clement.

"Behold I make the last things as the first,"[64] but the end transcends the beginning, because it fulfills it. This is why the return to the sources of Truth takes place by going backward, but especially by going forward: "We *remember* that which is to come." This amazing paradox of St Gregory of Nyssa corresponds to the liturgy, which "recalls the Parousia." St Maximus the Confessor explains its impact well: "One should not seek the principle by moving backward, but one should contemplate the goal that is ahead, in order to know in the end the principle that has been left behind: in this end which man was unable to know from the beginning."[65] Love is precisely this crucial point where the original fullness invokes the fullness to come. In the days of the Old Covenant, the saints were the kings and the prophets, but now Macarius the Great says, "men who are anointed with the heavenly unction become Christs according to grace, so that they too are kings, priests, and prophets of heavenly mysteries."[66] "They have died and been resurrected. From now on, they have a taste of the immortality to come."[67]

If the monk sublimates duration, time, the Christian couple initiates their transfiguration and their integration into eternity. A chaste marriage protects the heart from the "unclean flux" of temporality and its passions and transforms the unique being of the spouses into a shrine for the only Beloved and the point of departure for shared ascents toward the House of the Father.

The marriage-procreation concept of old was *functional*, subordinated to the cycles of generations and tending toward the coming of the Messiah. The nuptial marriage-priesthood is *ontological*, the new creation that saturates human time with eternity. Like monasticism, marriage is eschatological; it is the mystery of the "eighth day" and the prophetic figure of the Kingdom. Monastic asceticism and nuptial asceticism

[64]*The Epistle of Barnabas* IV. 13, trans. J. B. Lightfoot, *The Apostolic Fathers* (Grand Rapids, 1978), p. 140.

[65]PG 40:631D.

[66]*Homily* XVII. 1, trans. A. J. Mason, *Fifty Spiritual Homilies* (Willits, California, 1974), p. 142.

[67]John Climacus, *The Ladder of Divine Ascent*. Step 15, trans. Colm Luibheid and Norman Russell (New York, 1982), p. 186.

meet: "The one who has received the Spirit and is purified
. . . breathes the divine life."[68] The Spirit causes the priestly
love of husbands and the maternal tenderness of women to
germinate and also opens them up to the world in order to
set free every neighbor and lead them back to God.

"Woman will be saved by childbearing" (1 Tim 2:15).
One must hear the hidden message of this utterance: the
bringing to birth of a new aeon[69] beyond all biological fertility. This word refers before all else to the Nativity that
inaugurates the aeon of the Incarnation; it also commends
chastity as a universal value that ushers in the aeon of
eschatological holiness.

                              *   *   *

Fraudulent myths, dreadful alienations, and a vast and
hollow literature band together and conspire to disregard the
charisms and the meaning of love. A brief restatement is
needed in order to trace the great outlines of anthropology,
to define the calling of the royal priesthood of all believers
and *in the light of monasticism* to understand marriage as a
nuptial priesthood. Only by ascending to the thought of God
about man, to the astonishing dignity of the new creation, is
it possible to grasp the essence of the nuptial community.

---

[68]St Gregory of Sinai, *On the Contemplative Life.*
[69]The Greek word *aion* means "perpetuity," "an age," "the world" (in a
spatial sense), "the cycle" (an unbroken age).

1.

Anthropology

God is sovereignly free, a fascinating mystery (*mysterium fascinosum*), absolutely and for all eternity. "What may be known of God is manifest" but "men keep truth imprisoned in unrighteousness" (see Rm 1:18-19). But "the Holy Spirit fears no one and despises no one." This statement of St Symeon the New Theologian means that God is not a master, and that man is not a slave. God is Freedom and man is the child of this divine Freedom: according to the Fathers, man is the "play of God."

The more the sanctuary appears deserted and secularized, the stronger the human Yes to the sacredness of life, refined in the fire of a faith that is royally free. Militant atheists cooperate in their own way to purify the image of God. Their critique, while strangling on itself, opens spaces for the creative thought of Christian thinkers. If in past centuries man sought to escape from adulterated forms of established religion, today, where the modern world bears down on man with all its technical and political weight, it is in the unique sanctuary of the believing minority that man intuitively senses human dignity and freedom, for "where the spirit is, there is freedom." The Church is invited to present to man a "showing" (epiphany) of the true God.

It is not a question of reforms in the Church; as it is, the Church is a miracle and a sanctuary. It is a question of *metanoia*, a change of the being of every believer. It is because he is the repository of Pentecost that he is a sojourner on earth. *Homo viator*, he feels under his feet "three thousand fathoms of water," but he knows spots in this world where the weights are still heavy, for "there is only yes in God." The end of the age of Constantine signifies the end of the great historical bodies and the joyous era of the apostolic faith of the witnesses. Monasticism and the royal priesthood of the believers inaugurate the Christian synthesis of the last days.

The Philanthropy of God

At the request of a pagan who asked him, "Show me thy God," Theophilus of Antioch replies, "Show me yourself, and I will show you my God."[1] He means that man, "created in the image of God," reflects the divine mystery and that the two are unutterable. When God fashioned the man Adam, "He considered the Christ-man, the Christ who was one day supposed to be what was now this clay and this flesh."[2] The profound reason for the Incarnation does not come from man, but from God, from His desire to become Man and to make of humanity a Theophany, the beloved ground of His presence. The liturgical sense understands this superbly and calls God the philanthropist, the lover of man. His love is outstretched toward the highest degree of communion; with or without the Fall, God created the world to become Man therein so that man could become "god by grace," a participant in the conditions of the divine life, the immortality and the chaste integrity of His being.

The Constitution of the Human Being: The Spirit and the Flesh

Scripture knows nothing of the Greek dualism of two substances in conflict, of the body being the prison of the soul.

[1]Theophilus *To Autolycus*, Book I, chap II, trans. Marcus Doub, *The Ante-Nicene Fathers*, vol II (Grand Rapids, Rept 1977), p. 89.
[2]Tertullian, *Liber de carne Christi*, PL 2:802.

It knows of only the moral struggle between the desire of the Creator and the desires of the creature, between the standard holiness and sin-perversion. The conflict between carnal man (*homo animalis*) and spiritual man (*homo spiritualis*) takes place in the totality of the human being. An indivisible entity, an incarnated spirit, man essentially "participates in being," to such an extent that St Peter defines the goal of his life: "that you may become partakers of the divine nature" (2 Pt 1:4). As *homo viator*, in a "state of passage," he fulfills his resemblance, his affinity, with the divine, or indeed the demonic, through his participations; he leads the entire visible creation in one direction or the other.

The soul *vivifies* the body and makes of it a living flesh; the spirit spiritualizes the entire human being and makes of him a spiritual man. The spirit is not a third element—body, soul, spirit—but a qualifying principle. It expresses and manifests itself through the psychic and the corporeal by qualifying them in terms of its energies. Indeed, asceticism constitutes a vast culture, a true science whose aim it is to make the body and the soul transparent and submissive to the spiritual. By contrast, man can "quench the Spirit" (1 Th 5:19), cause the source of his life to dry up, have carnal thoughts and reduce himself to mere animal flesh, the flesh of the flood, the prey of hell.

The Biblical Concept of the Heart

The heart the Bible speaks of is not the same as the emotional center of the psychologists. The Jews thought with the heart. As a metaphysical center, it integrates all the faculties of the human being; reason, intuition, and the will are never strangers to the choices and sympathies of the heart (Reason and the reasons of the heart of which Pascal speaks). Radiating and penetrating everywhere, it is nevertheless hidden in its own mysterious depth. "Know thyself" is addressed above all to this secret heart: "Enter within thyself, and there find God, the angels, and the Kingdom," as spiritual men say.

"Who can understand the heart?" Jeremiah asks, and He

replies, "I, the Lord, search the mind and try the heart"
(Jr 17:9-10). This means God can penetrate to the obscure
sphere of the unconscious and the subconscious. St Peter
speaks of the "hidden man of the heart" (*homo cordis
absconditus*); it is at this unfathomable depth that the human
self is found. Its mystery, in the likeness of God, is well
indicated by the words of St Gregory of Nyssa: "Since the
nature of our mind evades our knowledge, it has an accurate
resemblance to the Superior Nature; in that it cannot be
explored, it shows the character of the Incomprehensible."[3]
To the hidden God, mysterious in His essence (*Deus absconditus*) corresponds his "image" (*homo absconditus*).

"For where your treasure is, there will your heart be also"
(Mt 6:21). Man is worth what the object of his love and the
desires of his heart are worth. The "Jesus prayer," called the
"prayer of the heart," makes of the heart the place of the
perpetual presence of Christ. The Gospel and asceticism assign
to the heart the hierarchical primacy in the structure of the
human being; it colors this structure with its health or with
its diseases. In contrast to Leonardo da Vinci, all knowledge
is the offspring of a great love. "I love, therefore I am" (*amo
ergo sum*) indicates an original intentionality, innate and as
if magnetized. "Thou hast made us for thyself, and our
heart is restless until it rests in thee," St Augustine confesses.[4]
"It is for thee alone that I live, speak and sing."[5] "God has
placed in the human heart the desire for Him,"[6] whence comes
this magnificent name that St Gregory gives to God, "Thou,
whom my soul loveth."[7]

[3]*On the Making of Man*, XI, PG 44:155; see *The Nicene and Ante-
Nicene Fathers*, series 2, vol. V (Grand Rapids, Rept 1979), p. 396.
[4]*Confessions* I. 1.
[5]Gregory of Nazianzus, PG 36:560A.
[6]St Maximus the Confessor, *Ambiguorum Liber*, PG 91:1312AB.
[7]St Gregory of Nyssa, *Homilia II in Cantica canticorum*, PG 44:801A. [The
book *From Glory to Glory: Texts from Gregory of Nyssa's Mystical Writings*,
ed. Herbert Musurillo, S. J., New York: St Vladimir's Seminary Press, 1979,
may be consulted—ed.]

The Human Person

The Trinitarian Foundation

The revelation of the person is *the event* of Christianity. It comes from above, from the Trinitarian dogma. Each divine Person is a mutual giving, subsisting in the other and in the *circumincession*[8] of the Three. In this being with (*co-esse*), the Person exists *for* the communion and exists essentially *through* it. Strictly speaking, a Person exists only in God. Man has the inborn nostalgia to become "a person"; he attains it only in communion, through participation in the Trinitarian personalism of God.

"Do, and by doing, become."[9] This is a philosophical formula that theology raises to another formula, "become by overcoming"; not *sum*, but *sursum*.[10] It is the unceasing transcendence of self toward the divine Thou, "each beginning begetting a new beginning."[11] At this level, our person, our "me," does not belong to us in our own right; we receive it in the order of grace that perfects it. St Maximus specifies this: "identity [with oneself, with one's iconic truth] by grace." The deepest "I," the element most personal and unique, is a *gift*.

The Christological Foundation

In the age to come, St John says, "we shall be like Him" (1 Jn 3:2). This is because man is modeled after his divine Archetype, Christ. Life in Christ, even from earth, brings about the passage from the natural being to the Christ-like being.

[8]*Circumincession* (in Greek, *perichoresis*) is the "compenetration" of the Three Divine Persons in the unity of their essence and of their life.
[9]Renouvier, *Le Personnalisme.*
[10]Gabriel Marcel, *Homo Viator: Introduction to a Metaphysic of Hope,* trans. Emma Crauford (Chicago: Regnery, 1951), p. 26; *Du refus à l'invocation* (Paris: Gallimard, 1940), p. 190.
[11]St Gregory of Nyssa, *On the Soul and the Resurrection,* PG 46:57B.

In Christ, the divine is united to the human, and the ground of their communion is the divine Person of the Word. In this communion, the human consciousness of Christ is placed inside the divine consciousness.

In man, it is his human person that is the ground of communion with the divine and it is inside his human consciousness that the divine consciousness is established: "We will come to him and make Our home with him" (Jn 14:23). This is what allows St Paul to say, "It is no longer I who live, but Christ who lives in me" (Ga 2:20), and to desire in his pastoral task that "Christ be formed in you," (Ga 4:19). Man "the Christ-bearer" (*Christophoros*) discloses himself as a "christophany," a manifestation of Christ.

The Realization of the Person

On the natural plane, consciousness of oneself is discovered and understood only through the mediation of the social sphere. Here every human being is an individual, a biological and sociological category. He is gifted with a psychological center of integration that causes the whole to revolve around the self. As an egocentrical center, he is tempted to shut himself up in individualism. This is a rudiment, it is but a potentiality of the person that does not yet go beyond the individual.

The person is a spiritual category. If the individual is an individualized part of the whole of nature, all of nature is, by contrast, enclosed in the person. The individual is a natural given, he is a citizen of the State and Society; the person is a member of the Kingdom of God, presupposing the transcendence of the natural toward a creative response to the call from God. "Man," St Basil said, "is a creature that has received the command to become god,"[12] which means, according to St Maximus, "to reunite through love the created nature [human] with the uncreated nature [divine grace]."[13] This is the personal, and always unique, mode of existence, reach-

---

12St Gregory of Nazianzus, PG 36:560A.
13*Ambiguorum Liber,* PG 91:1308B.

ing the state of the "new creature" in Christ. This is holiness. The individual and the person oppose each other in the same being as two attributes. Charles Péguy maintained that the individual is the bourgeois that every man carries within in order to master him. The individual of whom it is said that he has a "strong personality" is often no more than a "typical" impression of the *déjà vu,* that one can classify according to psychological types or distinctive patterns. A saint strikes us by his personal countenance, unique in the world. He has never been seen before.

Freedom

The will is a natural faculty that carries its own desires. This is why asceticism cultivates above all else the renouncing of self-will, the release from all necessities that come from nature. Freedom, on the other hand, springs from the person and makes of him the master of all passions and of all natural necessity. "God has honored man by granting him freedom so that the good belongs in its own right to him who chooses it,"[14] St Gregory of Nyssa declares. St Maximus the Confessor[15] goes farther. To him even the need to choose lacks something; the perfect one has moved beyond choice and creates the good. He produces his own reasons, instead of submitting to them. Thus the freest acts and the most perfect are those in which there is no longer a choice.[16]

This freedom is protected in its entirety even by grace, which touches the soul in secret without ever forcing it. "The Spirit begets no will that resists Him. He transfigures by deification [*theosis*] only the will that desires it."[17] A living project of God, man is called to decipher and, in this sense, freely to create his destiny. "Man was begotten according to freedom by the Spirit, in order to be able to be self-moving."[18]

[14]PG 36:632.
[15]*Opuscula theologica et polemica,* PG 91:16B.
[16]Cf. Louis Lavelle, *Traités des valeurs,* p. 155; *Les puissances du moi,* p. 325.
[17]St Maximus the Confessor, *Quaestiones ad Thalassium*: scholia, PG 90:281.
[18]*Ibid. Ambiguorum Liber,* PG 91:1345D.

St Antony[19] differentiates the three wills that confront one another in man: divine, human, and demonic. Human *autonomy* "encloses" man within himself; it is unstable and uncertain. *Heteronomy* is the demonic will, hostile to man. *Theonomy* is not a mere dependence or submission, but synergism, communion, friendship: "No longer do I call you servants . . . but I have called you friends" (Jn 15:15). Beyond the slave and the mercenary ethic, the Gospel proposes the ethic of the friends of God. It is precisely when our freedom and our way of acting are ensconced within the actions of God that they find the only condition in which they can fully blossom. Faith is never mere intellectual assent or blind submission, but fidelity of a person to the Person. These are the relationships of marriage and of its epithalamium; the Bible turns to these each time it deals with the question of the relations between God and man.

By declaring a fiat to the will of God, I identify myself with the desires of the beloved Being, and the will of God becomes mine: "It is no longer I who live, but Christ who lives in me." God asks man to fulfill the will of the Father as if it were his own. This is the meaning of the word, "Be perfect just as your heavenly Father is perfect." "God has first loved us" for no reason, and already in this love He has caused us to understand something of His divine freedom. He loves us freely, without any merit, and, by that, His love is already a gift that inspires and stirs up the freedom of our own response.

Sophia (the Wisdom of God), in her awesome imaginings, in the delights of the "divine play" (cf. Pr 8:31) with the children of men, can "imagine" only beings of her race, the gods: "You too are gods, sons of the Most-High," says the Lord. This is why, according to St Symeon the New Theologian, "God unites Himself only with gods." They have received as a gift something of their own, something that only comes from the free motion of their heart. Only this freedom, only this free love clothes man with the "wedding garment" of the divine espousals. At the height of his amazement, St

19*Philokalia* I.

Gregory of Nazianzus cries out: "In truth man is the play of God."[20]

It is because we are able to say, "Thy will be not done," that we can say Yes. But this Yes must be brought forth in silence and at the source of our being. She who pronounced it on behalf of all is the Virgin, the Mother of all the living, the life-giving Source. Her fiat does not only come from the pure and simple submission of her will; it is pronounced with her entire being as the expression of her thirst and the fruit of her prayer.

God does not give orders; He issues invitations and calls out, "Hear, O Israel." The decrees of tyrants are answered by secret resistance; the invitation by the Master of the banquet is answered with the joyous acceptance of "those who have ears." The elect is the one who freely opens his hand and receives the gift. "They shall come and sing aloud on the height of Zion, and they shall be radiant over . . . the grain and the wine . . . their life shall be like a watered garden" (Jr 31:12).

God has breathed freedom into these "earthen vessels," and has situated them in time. Unfinished created being presupposes a temporal margin where it can become and discover itself in the image of the free Existent. And if failure is possible, if the possibility of refusal is implied in the creative act of God, this is because the freedom of the "gods," their free love, constitutes the essence of the human person: "I will betrothe you to myself forever . . . and you will know Yahweh. I have loved you with an everlasting love, virgin of Israel" (Jr 31:1). And even in the utterance, "Be fruitful and multiply," one hears the call to the bursting forth of the new creature.

The Latin word *persona*, as well as the Greek *prosopon*, signifies "mask." Consequently, this term contains in itself an entire philosophy of the human person. It clearly demonstrates that an autonomous human order does not exist, since to exist is to participate in being or in nothingness. While participating, man can make of himself an "icon of God," or he can become a demonical grimace, an ape of God. Man's

---

[20]*Carminum liber* I: theologica, PG 37:771.

face possesses an orientation that determines him. In the Incarnation, God is no longer only God, He is God-man. Man,
too, is no longer only man, but man-god, a deified being. St
Gregory of Nyssa clearly states it: "Humanity is composed
of men with the face of angels and of men wearing the mask
of the beast."[21] "Until the end of his life" the spiritual man
"does not cease to add fire to fire."[22] Thus man can revive
the flame of love and exhibit the likeness; he can also light
the fire of Gehenna, erect the place of unlikeness, hell. He
can by a No break his being into infernal fragmentations and
solitudes, and he can convert his Yes into an infinity of unions.

The Image and Likeness of God

While summarizing the thought of the Church Fathers, so
infinitely rich and varied, it may be said that each faculty of
the human spirit (intelligence, freedom, love, creation) reflects the image, which is essentially the complete human
centered on the spiritual, whose distinctive characteristic it is
to go beyond himself in order to cast himself into the infinity
of God and to find there the alleviation of his nostalgia.
Holiness is nothing but an unquenchable thirst, the intensity
of the desire for God. St Gregory of Nyssa teaches that every
limit contains in its essence a beyond, its own transcendence,
and this is why the soul can rest only in the actual infinity of
God.[23] The saints are souls of longing.

This nostalgia is inborn, it is in germ at the time of the
first destiny, and the Church Fathers strongly emphasize that
Christ re-assumes and re-vivifies that which was interrupted
by the Fall. The image of healing is one of the most frequent
in the Gospel; it is even normative, since resurrection is the
cure for death. This is why creation presupposes the Incarnation, in order to cause the synergism of the acting of God
with man to progress and to guide man toward the day of

---

[21]De hominis opificio, PG 44:192CD.
[22]St John Climacus, Scala Paradisi, gradus I, PG 88:644A; The Ladder
of Divine Ascent, trans. Lazarus Moore (Boston, 1978), p. 10.
[23]De vita Moysis, PG 44:401B; [English translation by Abraham J. Mal-
herbe and Everett Ferguson, The Life of Moses (New York, 1978), p. 113.]

the Parousia, where the germ arrives at final maturation. The initial plan, *en arche* (in the beginning), coincides with its *telos* (completion), archaeology with eschatology. From the Edenic "tree of life" through the Eucharist where the fruit is given again, one turns "toward the table without veil," the banquet of the Kingdom.[24] From the initial perfection, fragile because it was unconscious, one moves toward conscious perfection, in the image of the perfection of our Father in heaven. The *image*, the objective foundation, calls for the subjective, personal *likeness*. The germ ("to have been created in the image") leads toward the blossoming: "to exist in the image" of the Existent. To "God is Love" corresponds man's *amo, ergo sum*. "The greatest event between God and the human soul is to love and to be loved."[25]

The Disease and the Cure

Before the Fall, animal life was outside the spiritual being of man; opened and turned toward him, it was awaiting its proper spiritualization-humanization (Adam's "naming" the beings and things). The fall of the sense faculties precipitated events, and animal life was added to the human being.[26] The Eastern Fathers specify that it is spiritual man—man in the image of God, the being supernaturally natural—who is primordial and normative, and that mere "natural" man was added to this "accidentally." The animal-biological element seems alien to the true nature of man, owing to its being appropriated *before* its spiritualization, *before* man had achieved power and the mastery of the spiritual over the material. The error is the result of a precocious and untimely identification. Clement of Alexandria detects original sin in the fact that "the first man of our race did not bide his time, desired the favor of marriage before the proper hour, and fell into sin by not waiting for the time of God's will."[27] Animal nature, good in itself, now constitutes man's down-

[24]Rv 22:1-2.
[25]Callistus Cataphygiotes, *De vita contemplativa*, PG 147:860AB.
[26]St Isaac of Syria, *Homilia* 3.
[27]*Stromatum liber* III. 14, PG 8:1193.

fall, on account of the perversion of the hierarchy of values.
"Nothing among creatures is evil except misuse, which comes
from the mind neglecting to cultivate itself as nature demands."[28] "It is not desire, but desire of such kind [concupis-
cence] that is evil."[29] It is the axiological faculty of apprecia-
tion, the spirit of discernment, that has been wounded;[30]
"removed from God, reason becomes brute-like, demonic:
estranged from its true nature, it yearns for what is alien to
it."[31]

Asceticism aspires to the true nature, to the "dispassionate
passion"; its struggle is never against the flesh, but against
the perversions of the flesh, against unlawful concupiscence
that is *against nature*. It is the source, the spiritual, that is
poisoned because the ontological norm was transgressed by
the spirit. For St Gregory Palamas, the passions arising from
nature are the least serious, since they only express the
gravity of matter due to its failed spiritualization. The source
of evil lies in the duplicity of the heart, where good and
evil are oddly side by side, "the workshop of righteousness
or of unrighteousness."[32] In terms of the "image," man always
seeks the absolute, but outside Christ the "likeness" remains
inoperative; sin perverts the intentionality of the soul and
the latter will seek the absolute in idols, will come to quench
its thirst in mirages, without being able to reascend to God.
Grace, reduced to the potential state, arrested in its outpour-
ing,[33] can no longer reach man except by the supernatural
path—supernatural not in relation to his nature, but in relation to his diseased, sinful condition. The truth of man ante-
cedes his duplicity; it becomes dominant again as soon as
man is placed in Christ. The vision from "below" must be
completed by the vision from "on high," which proves that

[28]St Maximus the Confessor, *The Third Century*, 4, PG 90:1017CD, trans.
Polycarp Sherwood, *St Maximus the Confessor. The Ascetic Life, The Four
Centuries on Charity*, Ancient Christian Writers n. 21 (1955), p. 173.
   [29]Didymus Alexandrinus (the Blind), *Fragmenta in Proverbia*, PG
39:1633B.
   [30]St Basil, *Homilia in Psalmum* XLIV, PG 29:408A.
   [31]St Gregory Palamas, *Homilia* LI.
   [32]St Macarius the Great, *Fifty Spiritual Homilies*, trans. A. J. Mason
(Willis, California: Eastern Orthodox Books, 1974), p. 122.
   [33]Metropolitan Philaret of Moscow, *Discourses and Sermons* I. 5.

sin is secondary, as is all negation. No evil will ever be able to erase the initial mystery of man, for there is nothing that can destroy in him the indelible imprint of God.

Studies in patristics stress the role of man's first destiny: "Through Christ the integrity of our nature is restored" because He "represents in form [Archetype] what we are,"[34] and, conversely, because in Christ we become like Him. The sacraments recreate the original nature of man, his Adamic integrity; the Holy Spirit is restored to us in the consecration of baptism and in the chrism of the anointing. Confession is a therapeutic treatment of purification, and the Eucharist introduces the leaven of immortality and of incorruptibility. Human nature is linked to the very power of the resurrection. One may say that the ascetic and the mystical life involve an ever growing awareness of the sacramental life. Their classic description by means of a single image, that of the mystic marriage, indicates the identical nature of the two.

The Liturgical Vocation of Man

In the liturgy of St John Chrysostom, the Cherubic Hymn ("We who mystically *represent* the Cherubim") shows the icon of the angelic ministry of adoration and of prayer in man. It is also the moment where the angelic hosts join the liturgical celebration. Man is associated with their song first in the *Trisagion* ("Holy God, Holy Mighty, Holy Immortal") and then the *Sanctus* resumes the theme of the Anaphora, the eucharistic praise of the Trinity. Men and angels are united in the same élan of adoration ("Holy, Holy, Holy, Lord God of Sabaoth. Heaven and earth are full of Thy Glory"). The content of the age to come, "full of glory," begins already on earth.

A saint is not a superman, but one who discovers and lives his truth as a liturgical being. The best definition of man comes from the Liturgy: The human being is the one of the *Trisagion* and of the *Sanctus* ("I will sing unto the Lord as long as I live"). St Antony speaks of a doctor who gave the

[34]St Gregory of Nazianzus, PG 37:2.

poor all that he did not need and sang the *Trisagion* all day long, uniting himself to the choir of angels.[35] It is for this "action" that man is "set apart," made holy. To sing to God is his one preoccupation, his unique "labor": "And there came from the throne a voice that said: 'Praise God, all you his servants' " (Rv 7:11). In the catacombs, the most frequent image is the figure of a woman in prayer, the *Orant;* she represents the one true attitude of the human soul. It is not enough to *say* prayers; one must become, *be* prayer, prayer incarnate. It is not enough to have moments of praise. All of life, each act, every gesture, even the smile of the human face, must become a hymn of adoration, an offering, a prayer. One should offer not what one has, but what one is. This is a favored subject in iconography. It translates the message of the Gospel: *chaíre,* "rejoice and be glad," "let everything that has breath praise the Lord." This is the astonishing lightening of the weight of the world, when man's own heaviness vanishes. "The King of Kings, the Christ is coming," and this is the "one thing needful." The doxology of the Lord's Prayer ("the kingdom and the power, and the glory") is the heart of the liturgy. It is to respond to his vocation as a liturgical being that man is charismatic, the one who bears the gifts of the Spirit, and the Holy Spirit Himself: "You have been sealed with the Holy Spirit . . . you whom God has taken for His own, *to make His glory praised"* (Eph 1:14). One could not state more precisely the liturgical essence and destiny of man.

Patristic meditation is forever oriented toward the liturgy, the *opus Dei.* "I go forward singing to you," St John Climacus cries joyously. The same cheerfulness radiates from the winged words of St Gregory of Nazianzus: "Your glory, O Christ, is man, whom you have stationed in this world like an angel, a crier of your splendor; it is for you that I live, for you that I speak; I have become a living oblation to you—the one talent that is left of all my possessions."[36] In the same vein, St Gregory Palamas writes, "Illumined, man reaches the eternal heights . . . and already here on earth he has become

[35]PG 65:84.
[36]*Carminum liber* II. historica, PG 37:1327.

a complete miracle. Even without being in heaven, he emulates the untiring singers of hymns; like another angel of God on earth, *he leads the entire created family to God.*[37] The Church is mystagogic. It graciously initiates man into the miracle, and offers it to all: "Gathered in Your temple, we see ourselves already in the light of Your heavenly glory." The best evangelization of the world, the most effective witness to the Christian faith, is this full liturgical hymn, the doxology which rises from the depths of the earth, in which moves the powerful breath of the Paraclete who alone converts and heals.

[37]*De mentali quietudine,* PG 150:1081AB.

2.

Marriage and the Monastic State

The One Absolute

A prayer of the sacrament of marriage asks, "Grant to these, Thy servants, chastity and mutual love in the bond of peace." Conjugal chastity and monastic virginity are contrasts that echo one another in their seeming antinomy. But the words of Christ, "Let the one who understands understand," apply to each of the two states; the one and the other are thereby situated on the level of the same ascesis of the Absolute.

There is no reason, except a pedagogic one for the masses, to call one path or the other the preeminent Christianity, since what is valid for all of Christendom is thereby valid for each of the two states. The East has never made the distinction between the "precepts" and the "evangelical counsels." The Gospel in its totality is addressed to each person; everyone in his own situation is called to the *absolute* of the Gospel. Trying to prove the superiority of one state over the other is therefore useless: it is an abstract, because impersonal, process. The renunciation at work in both cases is as good as the positive content that the human being brings to it: the intensity of the love of God.

St Paul's pastoral sense seeks the fulfilment of an "undivided service." The nuptial community, which is the "domestic church," and the monastic community shed light upon each other and help one another in this same service. Church doctrine has never lost sight of this balance. Councils and synods have defended it against the assaults of Manichaeism

65

and extreme spirituality. About 340, the Council of Gangra[1] condemned the Eustathians who said that no one living in a state of marriage had any hope toward God. By imposing severe penalties, even excommunication, upon the heretical disdain of the marriage bond, the Council reaffirmed the equilibrium between the various aspects of the same "mystery": "We have regard for continence, . . . [but at the same time] we honor the *holy companionship* of marriage." Yet, an entire literature of an ingratiating naivety still contrives to speak, for example, of the marital "omnibus" and the monastic "express" directly linking heaven to earth . . . And if holiness appears miraculously, it is evidently "in spite of marriage." The impressive argument mentions Revelation (14:1-5), a cryptic allusion to those who have "not been defiled with women." There is no decisive reason to state that it is a matter of physiological virginity. The Church absolutely forbids viewing the marriage union as a defilement. It is therefore not at all a question of the married state but of bodily prostitution in extramarital affairs or simply of the reality of concupiscence. The chastity of the virgins in this text is a gift of God and a spiritual way of being. Every other interpretation contradicts Church doctrine on the chastity of the married life. Suffice it to ask whether the Apostle Peter should be considered "defiled."

Upon discovering the splendor of love, how many do not believe that they should flee from the Church, confounding it with a bad apology and a simplistic theology. Belittling one estate in order to praise the other offers no profit. Patristic wisdom states it clearly: What merit would there be for an ascetic to renounce matrimony if marriage were an inferior state? The true comparison only renders more luster to one of the estates, illumined by the full light of the other.

John Chrysostom insists that the requirements of the Gospel are the same. Perfection in the image of the Father in heaven, the new commandment of love, and the beatitudes are addressed equally to every human being: "When Christ orders us to follow the narrow path, He addresses Himself not only to monks but to all men. Likewise He orders every-

---

[1]Canons I, IX, X, and XIV. Likewise, V and L of the *Apostolic Canons*.

one to hate his own life in the world. It follows from this that the monk and the layperson must attain the same heights, and if they fall they inflict the same wounds upon themselves." And further, "You are entirely mistaken if you think that there are certain things required of seculars, and others for monks . . . they will have the same account to render. . . . And if any have been hindered by the marriage state, let them know that marriage is not the hindrance, but their purpose which made ill use of marriage. Use marriage *chastely,* and you shall be the first in the Kingdom of heaven, and you shall enjoy all good things."[2]

Interiorized chastity depends on the structure of the spirit. And thus, numerous women sinners became "wise virgins" (St Mary of Egypt, St Pelagia). By contrast, while commenting on the parable of the ten virgins, the synaxarion of Great and Holy Tuesday treats the foolish virgins as sinners: it teaches us *not to rest as though safe in virginity.* Likewise, according to the *Philokalia,* numerous monks who sin in their heart "lose their virginity." The married as well as the monastic state are two forms of chastity, each one appropriate to its own mode of being.

Coventry Patmore, one of the few poets to deal with married love, says, "Those whose hearts are pure are virgins before God; marriage does not extinguish the vestal fire but makes its flame burn all the brighter; its praise is warm and living; and married lives faithful to the honor lying at the heart of love are fountains of virginity."[3]

Chastity signifies that one belongs totally to Christ, undividedly. For monks, it is an engagement of the soul in unmediated relationship, and for the spouses, engagement through the *hypostasis* of matrimony. This mediate character does not in the least diminish the value of the nuptial union. The spouses who comprehend this truth pray, "Grant, O God, that by loving one another we may love you."[4] If according to Nietzsche, "in true love, the soul encloses the body,"[5] then

[2]*Adversus oppugnatores vitae monasticae* III. 14.

[3]Trans. Ch. du Bos, in *Etudes Carmélitaines* (1935), p. 185.

[4]*Etudes Carmélitaines* (1939), p. 32.

[5]*Beyond Good and Evil.* For Swedenborg, "everyone becomes the image

in the charismatic love of marriage it is God who enshrines the one nuptial being. John Chrysostom explains this by saying that when love unites the spouses to unite them more fully to God, it "does not have its principle in nature, but in God," and "they are exactly like Jesus Christ who, united to his bride the Church, was not less one with the Father."[6]

Inspired by St John Chrysostom, Boukharev applies the monastic vows to marriage: "The essence of obedience, of chastity, and of poverty consists in the promise made before God and the Church to seek only that which is due to God, to His will, His grace, His truth. Poverty does not reside in total deprivation understood in a tangible sense (the physiological view), but in the spiritual use of all goods, according to grace; likewise, chastity requires devotion and undivided faithfulness to God, to His grace and His truth. One becomes a spouse to belong in nuptial love only to the Lord (vow of chastity), to be led only by the Lord (vow of obedience), and to have recourse only to God (vow of poverty)."

In marriage, the nature of man is changed sacramentally, as it is, though in another mode, in the one who becomes a monk. The deepest inner relationship unites the two. The promises exchanged by the betrothed introduce them in a certain manner into a special monasticism, because here too there is a dying to the past and a rebirth into a new life. Moreover, the rite of entrance into the monastic order makes use of nuptial symbolism (the terms "betrothed" and "spouse"), while the ancient marriage rite included the monastic tonsure, signifying the common surrender of the two wills to God. Thus, marriage includes within itself the monastic state, and that is why the latter is not a sacrament. The two converge as complementary aspects of the same virginal reality of the human spirit. The ancient Russian tradition viewed the time of engagement as a monastic novitiate. After the marriage ceremony, a retreat in a monastery was prescribed for the newly married to prepare for entrance into their "nuptial priesthood." The monastic atmosphere, so pro-

of his own love, even in external appearance," *Heaven and its Wonders,* trans. Samuel Noble (New York, 1885), p. 481.

[6]*Homily III on Marriage,* 3.

foundly linked to marriage in its very symbolism, only served to enhance the limpid joy of the wedding feast.

The Calling

All of mankind's depravities weigh heavily upon matrimony. Commonplaces or betrayals have transformed it into a grotesque caricature, summarizing all that is most trivial and odious in society. In public places and on the stage, a crowd hungry for unhealthy spectacles has torn away the nuptial veils. It is not easy to write an apology of marriage; it is easier to scorn it and to praise solitude or celibacy. A certain romanticism will always seek striking heroism and poeticized images. Looked at from the outside, the married life seems lacking in beauty and loftiness, and is basically prosaic. The faraway star of the hermits has always seemed bright in the eyes of those who are in need of a beacon. It was dangerous to praise love before regenerating fallen man. But the slothful servant, simply out of reaction, has allowed such a distance to establish itself that pagan eroticism has led directly to the legalistic disdain of marriage.

Thousand-year-old institutions, ancient habits of mentality, are crumbling nowadays at an astonishing speed. An all too masculine civilization leads the world to the brink of the abyss. The machismo myth, that of the stud, and the counter-myth of the liberated Amazon woman are dead-end streets. The "Godless" world is above all a world without the Virgin and without the maternal priesthood of the woman. In this emptiness, Nietzsche's words addressed to women take on a prophetic ring: "It is in your love that your honor is found; to always love more than you are loved, to always be first in love." In the struggle between spirituality and Soviet materialism, the scales of the religious victory leaned toward the side where woman had put the weight of her frail womanhood. The true feminine ingenuity was found in the spiritual. The veil, symbolic of mystery, hides the "little way" of the servants of God; consumed by their fiat, they are "God's smile" that saves the world.

The time has come to assert the fullness of matrimony, its state of grace, and to free the married conscience from the complexes imposed upon it. The true monk will rejoice in this, for he, more than anyone else, is able to discern the real value of marriage. Its path is narrow, perhaps the most narrow of all, since there are two that walk upon it.

The Martha type in the Gospel is usually understood as that of matrimony. However, neither this type nor that of Mary offers a solution to the conflicts of life. There is something stilted about both, in the manner of a thesis and an antithesis. The Mary type, in so far as it is absolute, cannot be lived in the world. The Martha type is not even desirable. Through this diptych (where Martha has been sacrificed somewhat) one can understand how well both types complement one another in a single face, Martha-Mary.

Being in the world, breathing its foul air, and "gaining Christ" at every moment of one's life; remaining at the feet of Christ without leaving the world; standing simultaneously before God but also before the world.

Marriage begins in joy, but as at the wedding of Cana, "the hour has not yet come." The wedding rite symbolically summarizes the entire married life. The betrothed have already exchanged rings; they have already been crowned and they partake of the one cup of life. It is only in the evening of life that this cup, symbolic of fullness, will be taken, when the shadow of the crowns will fall upon it. It is a slow and progressive birth. Léon Bloy would speak here of the spaces of the heart that do not exist as of yet but are created by suffering. In order to be loved by the other, one must renounce oneself completely. It is a deep and unceasing ascetic practice. The crowns of the betrothed refer to martyrdom. According to Tauler, then, "certain ones undergo martyrdom once by the sword; others know the martyrdom of love that crowns them interiorly." This is the *kenosis* (emptying, humbleness) proper to married life, the heroism of which is hidden under the garment of the day-by-day. At the time of their maturity, there are nuptial unions that evoke trees whose branches are "roots that drink from heaven"—to use Rilke's image; the common cup of tenderness, of the evening sacrifice (*sacrific-*

ium vespertinum), allows one to see, far off, "that nuptial contrasts are the poles on which the heavenly spheres revolve" (Coventry Patmore). Stripped of the attire with which the crowd had covered him, Eros lets the face of the Shulamite appear, crying with the Spirit, "Come, my Beloved!"

*   *   *

To an outside, superficial observer, marriage signifies sexual pleasure, and the monastic estate a physiological anomaly. The average person, bourgeois in spirit, has neither the desire nor the time to be interested in virginity and, by the same token, knows himself all too well not to despise his own married state in his innermost heart.

One must ascend to the sphere of the absolute to understand the full spiritual meaning of these two states. One mountain top can never be truly judged except from another, and the summit grows larger as one ascends a neighboring peak.

The true monk understands the qualitative difference that exists between matrimony and unchastity; inversely, the state of grace of true marriage makes one understand the qualitative difference between monastic virginity and the celibacy of which St Paul said, "It is better to be married than to be tortured"; the difference in each of these two states is not physiological at all, but that between grace and sin.

The Christian life is charismatic, which means service, *diakonia,* never domination, power, or superiority. Things are entirely different in the world: "This is not to happen among you; anyone who wants to become great among you must be your servant," and "the one who makes himself as little as this little child is the greatest in the Kingdom of heaven." The episcopacy bears witness to this, and is greatly praised in the beautiful words, "We are not the masters of your faith, but the servants of your joy."[7]

If vocations and spiritual gifts differ, all human beings are equal in that they have all been created, and they are all

[7] As quoted by Arnold, *La femme dans l'Eglise,* p. 77.

sinners who are equally powerless to enter the Kingdom of God on their own strength. They are equal in that they feel that a call has gone out to them; they equally share the unique, common "sadness of not being saints" (Léon Bloy, *The Poor Woman*). Greatness does not consist in being this or that, but in living up to one's ability, as determined by God.

If hesitancy arises over the path to follow, it is not the path as such that determines the choice, but the sense of a calling and of the gift. "Seek the Holy Spirit, fast, pray, give alms, and let everyone find out for himself what he must do." St Paul does not teach it any differently: "let everyone walk according to the part which the Lord has given him, according to the call he has received from God," "for everyone has received a particular gift from God, one this way, the other that way."

The lives of the saints teach us that when St Macarius, the great ascetic, lived in the desert, an angel appeared to him, ordering that he follow him to a remote town. Upon arriving there, he made him enter a poor dwelling where a humble family lived. The angel showed him the wife and mother of this household and told him that she had become a saint by living in peace and perfect harmony with all her family, since her marriage, in the midst of daily occupations, keeping a chaste heart, a deep humility, and a burning love for God. And St Macarius entreated God for the grace to live in the desert as this woman had lived in the world.

The aim of this story is not to set the monastic life against life in the world, and even less to classify them, but to show the positive value of each way of life, its own state of grace.

Before his death, St Paphnutius narrated all the things that God had revealed to him; he tells his disciples, "not to despise anyone in this world, even those committed to wedlock . . . because there is no state of life in which souls faithful to God are not found, and who perform in secret the actions that please him. This makes us see that it is not so much the profession that one chooses, or what appears to be most perfect in one's way of living, which is pleasing in his sight, but the sincerity and the disposition of the spirit."[8]

Monastic holiness and married holiness are the two faces of Tabor; the Holy Spirit is the limit of the one and the other. Those who reach the summit by either of these paths "enter into the peace of God, into the joy of the Lord"; the two ways, contrary to human reason, are found to be inwardly united in the end, mysteriously identical.

It is sufficiently clear by now that the best, and perhaps the only, method to fathom the value proper to matrimony is by comprehending the greatness of the meaning of monasticism. One will better understand the vocation of marriage in the light and the school of monasticism.

Monasticism

The first name that comes to mind is that of St Antony, the father of monasticism (born in Egypt, lived from about 250 to 350). Still an adolescent, his mind was captivated by the words of Christ: "If you wish to be perfect, go and sell what you own and give the money to the poor, and you will have a treasure in heaven; then come, follow me." How rich in meaning these words are: the call to perfection, the total renunciation of self, the oblation of self, the offering of one's being and life, the naked following of the naked Christ, as the great spiritual men said, and finally, the eschatological vision of a treasure in heaven, the passionate nostalgia of the Kingdom of God.

St Antony leaves the world, not as a dreamer pursuing an impossible dream, but by the thrust of the Holy Spirit; he goes deep into the desert, like Christ after His baptism: "I will lead him into the wilderness and speak to his heart" (cf. Ho 2:14). The words of Hosea emphasize something very direct, a freedom, an astonishing intimacy between God and the simple of heart. It is rather symptomatic that the early Desert Fathers did not want any rules, for fear of substituting the

---

[8]*Historia Monachorum.* See R. Flacelière, *Amour humain et Parole divine,* p. 185.

magnificent freedom of the Gospel for the law. There were no vows either, and it is only later, with the unavoidable democratization through the massive influx of people, that a uniform discipline was established in order to avoid abuses, and for the greater good of those who do not scale the heights (*qui non ascendunt ad sublimia*).

The second name is that of St Pachomius (253-346), a young soldier converted by a Christian community. His military past and his experience in the community make him the founder of the first regular monastic community. It is after his death that his disciples introduce the monastic vows for the first time.

St Basil (329-379) gives entire preference to "cenobitism," the monastic life in an organized community. It is characterized by:

1. The common possession of goods, in imitation of the apostolic communities;
2. The emulation of charity;
3. Poverty as the means of obtaining freedom of the spirit.

St Basil wrote monastic rules. (His *Moralia* are composed of quotations from Scripture that are grouped in chapters. The intention is clear: to follow the words of Christ step by step.) But one peculiarity should be noted: the monastic communities were directed by an abbot (frequently a simple monk) chosen by the monks themselves. This is the essentially charismatic character of monasticism, the vocation of which lies outside every priestly function. Priests play no role in the monastic life proper, except in the administering of sacraments.

*   *   *

Historically, monasticism is explained as the most radical opposition to the reign of evil in the world, by a categorical No to every compromise, every conformity. Its truly evangelical violence prescribed abandoning the confused, ambiguous forms of this world and suggested establishing a city of monks on the edge of this world. The nostalgia for the Kingdom of God was the reverse of the all-too-human nostalgia for the empire, which is called the Christian empire perhaps too hastily.

It should be noted, secondly, that in times of persecution the demonstration of the maximalism of the Christian faith, its testimony being planted like a thorn in the world's flesh, belonged to those martyrs the Church venerates like its own heart and calls the "wounded by the love of Christ." The martyr preaches Christ by giving himself as a "spectacle" before God, the angels, and men; he becomes a living, and very striking, symbol of total faithfulness to Christ. Origen addressed a rather cruel remark to us by saying that a time of peace is propitious to Satan, who steals from Christ His martyrs and from the Church its glory. There is a special presence of Christ in the soul of the martyr, in his living configuration of Christ crucified. "Can you drink the chalice that I must drink?" our Lord asks the apostles. The apostles drink it in turn. According to this passage, the life of the martyr becomes conformable to the eucharistic chalice. Following the most ancient tradition, every martyr at the moment of his death follows the destiny of the good thief on the right, and enters immediately into the Kingdom.

Constantine's concordat installs the Church in history and offers it a legal status and an existence that is "peaceful" because it is protected by the laws of the state. From then on, the testimony that the martyrs rendered to "the one thing needful" and to the ultimate of existence passed to monasticism and is transformed there into the charismatic ministry of eschatological maximalism. The monastic estate will be viewed as a second baptism. Thus the "baptism of ascesis" replaces the "baptism of blood" of the martyrs.

The celebrated *Life of Antony,* written by St Athanasius, describes this father of monasticism as "the first who had attained holiness without tasting martyrdom."

The one who answers the Gospel's call to perfection becomes equal to the apostles, St Simeon explains. Like John the Evangelist, he can turn to the people and tell them

what he has seen in God. He can and he must. He cannot do
otherwise. A monk is a preeminent witness of the last things,
an apostle of the evangelical perfection. The dangerous
Thebaid, cradle of so many giants of the Spirit, the arid and
burning desert, was illuminated by their light. These astonishing masters of experimental knowledge taught the refined art
of living the Absolute of the Gospel. In the silence of their
cells, in the school of these "theodidacts" taught by God, the
birth of the new creature was slowly effected. One can say
that at least here, confronted with the world's compromises,
the *metanoia* of which the Gospel speaks, this reversal of the
entire economy of the human being, this metamorphosis into
a second birth, had succeeded.

Is it the indomitable opposition of the desert to the empire?
It is possible to see in it an opposition, a striking contrast, but
not a break. The two ways of living, in the world and at the
edge of the world, appear complementary; ideally they
culminate in the same reality, the one justifying the other, in
order to respond to the fullness that the Incarnation carried
in its wings. The monks leave this world to bless it forthwith
in the desert and to carry it in unceasing prayer. It is precisely
in the maximalism of the faith of the monks that the world
finds its true measure, the scale of comparison, the "canon of
life," the salt that destroys the insipid. By aspiring to the impossible, monasticism saves the world from the most dreadful
sufficiencies: belief in self (*autopistie*), self-sufficiency (*auto-
rythmie*), and adoration of self (*autolatrie*). In the formation
of the Christian type, which cuts through all sociological
types, in the very newness of the "new man," monastic
asceticism has played a decisive pedagogic role. Its spirit of
prayer and adoration, the discernment of spirits, its cultivation of spiritual attentiveness, its strategy of "unseen warfare"
with the demonic powers, its knowledge of the human heart
and the mastery of the spiritual over the corporeal reach an
astonishing level of perfection and become the "mirror of
conscience" to which the world can come and see itself. The
road, however, was covered with precipices. One had to
transcend the easy disdain for the human, and, by starting
with asceticism, rehabilitate matter, the body, the flesh of the

Resurrection. Contrary to the accepted view, a monk is not someone who diminishes his being, but one who expands it, who truly exists in the image of the Existing. It is very important to understand that asceticism is not at all a "philosophy of virtue," even less a "system of virtues," but the experimental participation, the unceasing communion, with the "wholly Other." This is why John Climacus constantly tells that what is proper to a monk is the unwearying love for God, whom he should love as a fiancé loves his betrothed. According to his disciples, he himself "inflamed by divine love was nothing but unceasing prayer, nothing but inexplicable love for God." The Desert Fathers never ceased reiterating that no asceticism, no private knowledge of love, comes close to God. True monasticism, however, never leads to isolation, since its task is not to unite man to the Holy Trinity, but to express its human truth among men.

* * *

By the words, "if you want to be perfect, sell what you have," the monks understood, "sell all that you are." This is the total oblation of one's own being. After giving all that one has, one offers all that one is. It is the "one thing needful" of the Gospel that makes of the monks "the violent ones who lay hold of the Kingdom," those who bear testimony to the last things and already live the "little resurrection." This is why in the days of the Church Fathers, apostolicity does not point to specialized missionary activities; the expression "apostolic man" describes the charismatic who, upon God's call, brings into being the promises of the Gospel of Mark (16:17-18). Man had fallen below himself, but asceticism elevates him above himself and gives him back his human dignity, an astonishing one, that of a new creature in Jesus Christ. It is the miracle at the wedding of Cana, the classical image of the metabolism of the human being; it is the metanoia, the second birth, the very real death and the still more real resurrection. "Let all things be new," St Paul exclaims. Concerning the meaning of being stripped in baptism, Nicholas Cabasilas writes, "We now approach to the true light, taking nothing with us . . . we proceed from the 'garments of skin' and show that we return by the same way and hasten to the royal garment. . . . So this water destroys the one life and brings the other into the open."

Gregory of Nyssa speaks of another humanity; for him, the person who is not moved by the Holy Spirit is not a human being. The magnificent meaning of monasticism lies precisely in this dynamism, this violence, this maximalism that aspires only to the ultimate, to the "foolishness" of which St Paul speaks. Whereas common sense declares, "God does not demand that much," monasticism proclaims *urbi et orbi* (to the entire world), "God is to be feared in his jealousy; He demands everything and does not rest."

Is this the Titanism of natural forces? Once more, faced by such numerous misunderstandings, one should return to the sources. According to the ascetics, the "virtues" are not different from the human dynamism set in motion by the presence of God. The Fathers distinguish between freedom, or the freedom of *intention,* and the freedom of deeds. They affirm the freedom to desire salvation, and leave its actual functioning entirely to God. To a certain degree, however, this desire is already operating because it corresponds to the desire of God to save the soul, and it thereby attracts grace. "I believe, Lord. Help thou my unbelief." To every sigh, each effort of the creature to transcend itself, corresponds the grace that carries it. This is the precise meaning of the words of Maximus the Confessor: "Man has two wings, freedom and grace." In its very principle, grace is the matrix of the human fiat, but it is only given to our total offering. "It is still God who puts virtues in the human heart," but to man belong "the hard labor and the sweat."

One could say, paradoxically, *"It is God who works, and man who sweats."* There is no question here of any "meritorious" work, but of human action within the divine action— this is the most precise definition of synergism. There is never a question of any reward. "God is our creator and savior; He is not the one who measures and weighs the price of our works" (Mark the Ascetic). "If God regarded merits, then no one would enter the Kingdom of God." It is God who works in us virtue, knowledge, victory, wisdom, goodness, and truth," Maximus clearly states. Every truth, however, is always paradoxical, antinomic. That is, the soul tends not toward *salvation* (in the "salvationist" sense of personal redemption) but toward the response that God expects from man. At the center of the immense drama of the God of Scripture (who is not exactly the same as the God of the theologians, since God can never be limited by a doctrine) is not only the interaction of grace and sin, the judge and the judged, but above all and essentially the *Incarnation,* the encounter and communion of the descending love of God and the ascending love of man. If it is necessary to save anything in this world, it is above all this love that God has given first to man, a love that surpasses, amazes, and unsettles us. The texts of the liturgy refer to it by a name that is already full of grace: the man-loving God (*theos philanthropos*).

* * *

Contrary to all romantic sentimentality, all "inner music," all psychism, the ascetic endeavor is sober, stripped of everything sentimental; each healthy emotion is severely screened. It removes every visual or sensory phenomenon and excludes all emotiveness: "If an angel appears to you, do not accept the vision. Humble yourself and say, 'I am not worthy to look at it.' " To Satan who had taken on the form of Christ, a monk declares, "I have no desire to see Christ in this world, but elsewhere, in the world to come." "Do not strive during prayer to discern any image or figure," Nilus of Sinai says. The method is the interiorization of the spiritual life oriented toward the indwelling in the Johannine sense: "We will come to him and make Our home with him." For the baptized, Christ is the *inner reality of existence.* Without abolishing the hiatus, the divine being fills man with His presence, through His unseen but burning proximity: "If you are pure, heaven is within you, and it is within you that you will see light, the angels, and the Lord." What is on high and at the beginning comes to be located in the heart of man, after the Incarnation.

The monastic life is fully explained by the thirst for God.
If one should wish to define it, one can say that it lies in the
degree of intensity of this desire, this thirst for God. This
is why humility is above all the power that locates the axis of
our life in God, and destroys most radically every spirit of
resentment or of egocentrism. It is also the art of being precisely in one's place. The Gospel leaves us two images: that
of the friend of the Bridegroom, and that of the servant of
the Lord.

In the unseen warfare waged by the ascetics, attention is
drawn to the spiritual source of evil. Sin does not come from
below, but from above, from the spirit, the fallen angel. This
is why asceticism is the mastery of the spiritual over the
material and the psychic, without destroying anything in them.
Ascetic culture creates the perfect balance; it is never a mere
destruction of the passions, but their healing and their transformation. A true ascetic is a passionate lover of God and
His creature.

Seen from below, the ascetic life is an unceasing struggle.
Seen from above, it is the progressive illumination of the
human being, his "spiritualization" (the penetrating *pneuma*)
by the energies of the Holy Spirit. "Purify us from all stain;
come and dwell within us," the Church prays.

The ascetic begins with a vision of his own human condition, for "no one can know God unless he first knows himself." "The one who has seen his sin is greater than the one
who raises the dead." "He who has seen himself is greater
than he who has seen the angels." Thus the ascetic life introduces us to the perfect understanding of the damages caused
by evil in the human soul, and represents some type of ascetic
scaphander (diving suit) to make the descent and explore
its caverns peopled by monsters. (Psychiatrists and psychologists pay much attention nowadays to the ascetic writings.)

After taking this dreadful "snapshot" of its own abyss,
the soul aspires to divine mercy. "From the abyss of my
iniquity, I invoke the abyss of your grace." The ascent is
gradual. Without attempting an impossible "imitation" of
Christ, the monk follows him inwardly: "Purity of heart is
love for those who fall." The soul is gladdened, opens wide

into a cosmic charity, and despoils itself of all judgment. "The one who is purified sees the soul of his neighbor," "no one appears before him impure" and "if you see your brother in the act of sinning, throw about his shoulders the mantle of your love." It is the passage from fear to love: "The perfect reject fear, disdain rewards, and love with their whole heart." "What is the charitable heart?" Isaac of Syria asks. "It is a heart inflamed with charity for the entire creation, for men, birds, beasts, evil spirits. Moved by infinite pity, it even prays for reptiles." At this level, there is no question of acquiring knowledge about God: "Knowledge becomes love." "Love is God who throws His arrow, His only begotten Son, after having moistened its threefold point with the vivifying Spirit; the point is faith which not only introduced the arrow but the archer with it."[9] God enters the soul and the soul emigrates to God.

The Ascetic Monasticism of Every Believer

Since its advent, monasticism has been an integral part of the Church, because it expresses a spiritual norm that is *universal*, a normative value for *every* believer. The monks "lead the apostolic life according to the Gospel"; they are none other than "those who desire to be saved," who take seriously the call to the "one thing needful," of which the Gospel speaks, and therefore "do themselves violence in everything" (Nilus of Sinai). The one thing that remains is to make this fundamental aim suit the conditions of all and everyone.

According to *Novella* 133 of Justinian, "the monastic life is a sacred thing." Asceticism is not a system of merely moral rules, but a system of exercises implying spiritual gifts that is offered to every Christian life, as Cyril of Jerusalem explains. In his Rules,[10] St Basil compares the monks to the "violent ones" of the Gospel who "lay hold of the Kingdom," and thereby give expression to the maximalism of the Christian way of life.

---

[9]St Gregory of Nyssa, *Homilia IV in Cantica canticorum*, PG 44:852AB.
[10]*Sermo de renunciatione saeculi*, PG 31:632.

However, it is in its total, natural powerlessness, recognized and lived as a free and joyful oblation, that asceticism seeks and encounters God. The entire technique of the ascetic struggle centers on this receptiveness: "Behold, I stand at the door and knock; if anyone hears my voice and opens the door, I will come in to him and eat with him, and he with me" (Rv 3:20). This passage of a clearly eucharistic nature is easily applied to the Liturgy or to the internalized Eucharist, to unceasing communion. According to the great mystics, a Christian is a miserable person, a beggar of grace, who discovers the One who is still more miserable, more of a beggar, God Himself, begging for love at the door of man's heart. A Christian, then, is someone who listens and opens the door; from the meal of shared poverty the banquet of the Kingdom springs forth.

The soul only reaches full maturity by ceaselessly transcending itself toward the Other, when it no longer belongs to self. Humility-obedience creates in us the configuration of Christ crucified: it is the radical laying aside of each appropriation of grace and the Spirit. The anticontemplative tendency contrasts Eros to Agape[11] and confuses inwardness with being self-centered. For Gregory of Nyssa, however, Eros flowers into Agape and into love of neighbor: Eros is "the intensity of Agape."[12] "God is the Father of Agape and Eros." The two are complementary: Eros, moved by the Spirit, goes out to meet divine Agape. This allows Maximus the Confessor[13] to institute the equivalent of the monastic life for laypeople living in the world—for the monks contemplation, for the active laity the unceasing feeling of an unseen closeness. Moreover, to the question about action or contemplation, St Seraphim of Sarov replies: "Acquire inner peace, and a multi-

---

[11]Anders Nygren, *Eros et Agape* (Gütersloh, 1937). [English translation by Philip S. Watson, *Agape and Eros* (New York: Harper & Row, 1969).]

[12]*Epitetamene agape eros legetai,* St Gregory of Nyssa, *Homilia XIII in Cant. cant.,* PG 44:1048C. Agape alone would repress all loving return, every encounter between two subjects.

For the Fathers, Agape and Eros are two correlative expressions of divine love. Eros expresses the transrational, ecstatic aspect of Agape. For St Maximus the Confessor, Christ is Eros crucified.

[13]*Capitum de charitate centuria* II, III, PG 90:985AB, and 1041D.

tude of men will find their salvation near you." The great
merit of universalizing and popularizing the monastic method
so that everyone could discover its equivalent belongs to
Nicholas Cabasilas, layman and great liturgist of the fourteenth century. His treatise on the sacraments bears the telling
title *The Life in Christ.* In this sacramental and liturgical
aspect of the Church, he shows the heart of the mystical
experience for all, the secret of living in God that the Church
offers to all and everyone.

Universal Interiorized Monasticism

It is now possible to put the undying values of monasticism
into perspective. Through the dialectic of interiorization, they
can be established as principles for every Christian life. One
could easily show that the monastic vows of obedience,
chastity, and poverty are rediscovered in the life of every
Christian.

Total *obedience* to God supplants all self-sufficiency, every
ascendancy coming from the world. The one who truly obeys
God has dominion over the world, is royally free, and fully
enjoys the dignity of a king.

Chastity is found in the structure of the spirit and in the
priestly sacrifice of one's having and one's being; it is the
dispossession and the full consecration of one's life.

Poverty is a poor person's completely open sensitivity to
the designs of God and their prophetic penetration—who only
wants to know and to follow the Word in the world, who
hopes for one possession only, that of the indwelling of the
Spirit.

Prayer, as an unwavering state of the soul, becomes flesh
and miraculously transforms every task, every word, each
action into prayer, a living sign of the presence of God, the
ministry of praise.

Eschatological maximalism is the violence that lays hold
of the Kingdom, this totalitarianism of faith that seeks only
the one thing needful, transforming the world into the
Kingdom and its justice: in the light of the End, it sees and

contemplates "the flame of things." It is an existential attitude
tending toward the ultimate; it can only be an active waiting,
a preparation for the Parousia. Through his very life, the
person shows what he has seen in God. He does it and he
cannot do otherwise. It is in the human witness that the
Kingdom is present already; he announces it even through
his silences.

3.

The Royal Priesthood of the Believers

The Functional Priesthood of Ordination and the
Ontological Priesthood of the Believers

The anointing (1 Jn 2:20), formerly reserved for kings, priests, and prophets, is extended in the Church to all believers. It is no longer the ethnic element (Israel) or the spatial (the temple of Jerusalem) that constitutes the body (Jn 4:21-24); it is Christ who unites in Himself all those baptized "into the people of God," where everyone is a *layperson,* belonging to "the priestly people."

It is not a question of "priest" in the sense of "a presbyter" and of his sacramental power (the bishop). A priest of the royal priesthood (every believer) is one who participates in the Priesthood of Christ, not through his sacred functions but by virtue of his sanctified being. It is in view of this *ontological sacerdotal dignity* that each baptized person is sealed with the gifts, "anointed by the Spirit" in his very being. Attention must be drawn to the *priestly being* of every believer. This means that the believer offers the totality of his life and being as a sacrifice, that he makes of his life a liturgy. Every layperson is the priest of his existence.

The sacrament of the anointing by chrism (called confirmation in the West) is the sacrament of the universal priesthood; it puts all those who are baptized in the same priestly order, under the same sanctifying grace of personal holiness. From this perfect equality, some are chosen and installed as bishops and priests, always by a divine act. There is a difference of ministries within the priestly body. The ministry of the priest is *functional;* there is *no ontological* difference between clerics and laypeople. Without break or confusion, the priestly body seems to be structured and differentiated—but these are ministries of function, not of being, which renders every "lay" character of the members of the Church nonexistent, even impossible.

The Letter of Clement of Rome to the Corinthians (*ca.* 95 A.D.) mentions the "rules for laymen" binding the people (chapter 40). With St Cyprian in North Africa (third century), the term "lay" appears for the first time alongside that of "cleric." Opposite the clergy, the ones set apart for *the things of God,* the laypeople, are simple those who look after *the things of this world.* According to Jerome, these are the ones who marry, carry on business, cultivate the land, wage war, and testify in court. The first disquieting signs appear as early as the fourth century. It was the laypeople themselves who betrayed their dignity as priests, who became impoverished and divested themselves of their priestly essence. Then the bishops inevitably became more the center of gravity of the sacred, of the sacerdotal, of the "consecrated." A distance was formed by the indigence, the impoverishment, of the laity by its tragic refusal of the gifts of the Holy Spirit. The "treason of the laity" is certainly an abdication, a very strange alienation from their priestly nature. It is to this state of decadence that the pejorative terms of *biotikoi* (worldly) and *anieroi* (unholy) are applicable, referring to those who live in the world and are strangers to sacred realities. The artificial and false contrast between the laity and the clergy ends in a purely negative view, one that lacks all meaning: a layperson is one who has no ecclesiastical function. But the sacrament of anointing establishes everyone in a churchly function. The *Epistle to Diognetus* (end of the second century) speaks of Christians as "foreigners living in their native land. They remain on earth, but they are citizens of heaven."[1] They live essentially in the things of God.

[1]*The Address to Diognetus* 5. 10, trans. Edgar J. Goodspeed, *The Apostolic Fathers* (New York, 1950), p. 278.

The Sacrament of the Anointing with Chrism and its Three Dignities

The prayer found at the heart of the sacrament of anointing asks the seal of the gift of the Holy Spirit and specifies its aim: "That it may please him to serve Thee in every act and every word." This is the consecration, the complete placing of one's entire life in the ministry of the royal priesthood. Its absolute character stands out clearly in the rite of tonsure, a rite that is identical with that performed for one entering the monastic order. The eschatological intent reinforces the integrity of the consecration: "May he render Thee glory and may he have all the days of his life the vision of the joys of Jerusalem." The anointings with chrism are accompanied by the formula, "the seal of the gift of the Holy Spirit," and symbolize the fiery tongues of Pentecost. In his prayer over the holy chrism, the bishop asks, "O God, mark them with the seal of the immaculate chrism; they will bear Christ in their heart, in order to become a dwelling of the Trinity." Sealed with the Spirit, the person becomes a Christ-bearer, *Christophoros*, so as to be a temple "filled with the Trinity."

"Go and teach all the nations." These words of the Gospel read during the sacrament are addressed to each baptized person. Their call means that alongside the missionaries specially accredited by the Church every confirmed-anointed person is a missionary, an "apostolic man," in his own way. It is through his entire life as an interiorized liturgy and a Trinitarian dwelling, it is through his entire being that every layperson is called to give unceasing testimony. It is even to this end that he is entirely consecrated.

The laity forms an ecclesial abode which is, at the same time, of the world and of the Church. Laymen do not have access to the means of grace (the power of celebrating the sacraments); on the other hand, their sphere is "the life of grace," its penetration into the world. This is the "cosmic liturgy" in the world, already at work by the simple presence of "sanctified beings," of "Trinitarian dwellings." This is the apostolate and the mission through life, through the priestly essence which by its very nature drives out every profane and demonic element from the world. It is through the human in all its forms, through the social, that laypeople bring "the trisolar light," the lived dogma, the grace received and offered to the world.

"O Savior, you have given grace to the prophets, the kings, and the pontiffs. Give it also to those who receive the anointing," the bishop prays. The Fathers stress this threefold power of every believer: royal, priestly, and prophetic.

Macarius warns every baptized person that "Christianity is no ordinary thing . . . thou art called to kingly dignity." "Spiritual men, who are anointed with the heavenly unction, become Christs according to grace, so that they too are kings, priests, and prophets of heavenly mysteries."[2] But in the life of every man, what does it mean to be king, priest, and prophet? "What does the world think of?" Pascal asks. "Of dancing, waging war, ruling, without giving a thought to what it means to be a king and a man."

The Royal Dignity

In the Syriac anaphora of John Chrysostom, the priest asks for "a pure spirit that would make us strive for royal splendor." The direct meaning of this prayer alludes to ascetic mastery, the freedom from all ascendancy coming from the world, from the many forms of concupiscence, from all demonic powers. "Here comes Satan—but he has no power over me." This is the free word of a king. By this power of grace, which transforms his nature, man can say, "I have dominion over my instincts, I rule over the flesh and all the cosmic impulses." "Kings, by the ascendancy over our passions," as St Ecumenius has said it.[3] And St Gregory says, "The soul shows its royalty by the free dispositions of its desires; this is inherent only in a king. To dominate all is characteristic of a royal nature."

[2]*Homily* XXVII. 4, PG 34:696BC; *Homily* XVII. 1, PG 34:624BC, trans. A. J. Mason, *St Macarius the Great: Fifty Spiritual Homilies* (Willis: Eastern Orthodox Books, 1974), p. 202, 143.

[3]*Commentarium in Epist. II ad Corinthios,* PG 118:932CD.

However, every freedom *from* is at the same time a freedom *for*. If freedom is the "how" of human life and existence, it invites us to move to the "what" of life, its positive content, and leads us to the priestly dignity.

The Priestly Dignity

In its ultimate depth, the created being appears not only as "thought," but also as something loved. "God loved us first," St John says, and it is in this love that man truly becomes an existing being.

Created in the image of the Trinity, man is, in his essence, communion; this is why the organism of the Church, responding to this nature, is never an institution imposed from without, but the very truth of man, engraved in his nature, and showing him as a human being-church, a liturgical human being.

When man views himself on the level of his own mystery, he sees himself as a communion open to the world. The art of the great spiritual masters teaches that one should not be what one has, placing the self among one's possessions but one should own what one *is*, reducing all possessions to one's own being. We must always pass from *having* to *being*. It is not enough to "have poverty"; one should become poverty. "Blessed are the poor in spirit" perhaps signifies: the blessed are not those who have the spirit, who are owners of possessors of the spirit, but the blessed are those who *are* spirit. It is here that we touch upon the change of nature wrought by the sacrament, which renders nature priestly.

In Romans 12, St Paul admonishes us to offer our bodies as a living sacrifice, which is the "reasonable offering"; the reference to "cult" indicates the eucharistic sacrifice. The Epistle to the Tarsians (fourth century) says, "Honor those [who continue] in virginity, as the priestesses of Christ." Likewise, Minucius Felix (second century) observes that "he who snatches man from danger slaughters the most acceptable victim. These are our sacrifices, these are our rites of God's

worship."[4] Origen very clearly links the grace of the anointing
to the priestly offering of their life by the believers:

> All those who have received the anointing are priests
> . . . each one carries his sacrifice within himself, and
> he himself puts the fire on the altar so that he becomes
> a continual sacrifice. If I renounce everything I own,
> if I carry my cross and follow Christ, I have made an
> offering on God's altar. . . . If I love my brothers even
> to give my life for them, if I fight for truth and justice
> even to death, if I mortify myself . . . if the world is
> crucified to me and I to the world, I have offered a
> sacrifice on God's altar and I become the priest of my
> own sacrifice.[5]

It is a matter of the ascetic *katharsis* (purification), preparing for the state of *being a victim.*[6] Gregory of Nazianzus
describes the correct liturgical attitude in these words: "No
one can participate in the sacrifice unless he has offered himself as a victim."[7] "We are kings by dominion over our
passions; priests, by immolating ourselves as a spiritual host."[8]
John of Damascus[9] recalls the sword that pierces the heart of
the Theotokos (Lk 2:35), and applies to it the term "ointment poured forth" (Sg 1:3).

During the Liturgy, the officiating priest, while presenting
the offering, says, "Thine own of thine own we offer unto
Thee." The believer of the royal priesthood continues this
act *extra muros;* he celebrates the Liturgy through his everyday life, thereby replying to the prayer of the sacrament,
"That it may please him to serve Thee in every act and every
word." His presence in the world is like a continuation of the
epiclesis, an invocation of the Holy Spirit upon the day ahead,

---

[4]*The Octavius,* chap. XXXII, trans. Robert Wallis, *Ante-Nicene Fathers,*
vol. IV (Grand Rapids, Rept 1979), p. 193.
[5]*In Leviticum homilia* IX, PG 12:521-522.
[6]Under exceptional circumstances the Canons of Hippolytus bestowed the
dignity of the priesthood upon confessors who had not received the sacrament
of Holy Orders.
[7]Gregory the Theologian, *Oratio II Apologetica,* PG 35:498.
[8]From an anonymous sixth-century MS.
[9]*Homilia II in nativitatem B. V. Mariae,* PG 96:693B.

upon the work and the fruits of the earth, upon the work of the scholar whose eye has been purified by prayer. The pure in heart will see God, and through them God will make Himself visible.

The Prophetic Dignity

According to Scripture, a prophet is one who is aware of "the designs of God" in the world, one who interprets and announces the will of God, the inexorable advance of His grace.

In his *Proof of the Gospel*,[10] Eusebius of Caesarea writes concerning the anointing to the priesthood, "We burn the prophetic perfume in every place and we sacrifice to Him the fragrant fruit of a practical theology." This is an excellent definition of the laity in its prophetic dimension. Every member of the royal priesthood discloses a living, theophanic theology. We are, as St Ecumenius adds, "kings, by dominion over our passions; priests, to immolate our own bodies; prophets, as being fully informed of the great mysteries."[11] And in the same ultimate sense, "prophet, because he sees what eye has not seen," as St Theophilact says.[12]

Through the greatness of its confessors and martyrs, Christianity is messianic, revolutionary, explosive. In the domain of the caesar, we are ordered to seek and therefore to find what is not found there, the Kingdom of God. This means precisely that we must change the structure of the world, transform its passing figure. To change the world means to pass from what the world does not yet possess— for this reason it is still the world—to that into which it is transfigured, thus becoming another thing, the Kingdom.

This is the central and ultimate appeal of the Gospel, the call to Christian violence that lays hold of the Kingdom. John the Baptist is not just a witness of the Kingdom; he already is the place where the world is conquered and the Kingdom

[10]*Demonstrationis evangelicae liber secundus*, PG 22:92-93.
[11]*Comment. in Epist. II ad Corinth.* 2, PG 118:932CD.
[12]*Expositio in Epist. II ad Cor.*, PG 124:812.

is present. He is not only a voice that proclaims; he is its
voice. He is the friend of the bridegroom, the one who decreases and becomes transparent so that the Other may appear
and increase. This, then, is the prophetic dignity, to be someone who, by his life, by what is present within, proclaims
Him who is to come.

The New Holiness

It appears that a new spirituality is dawning. It aspires not
to leave the world to evil, but to let the spiritual element in
the creature come forth. A person who loves and is totally
detached, naked to the touch of the eternal, escapes the con-
trived conflict between the spiritual and the material. His
love of God is humanized, and becomes love for all the creatures in God. "Everything is grace," Bernanos wrote, because
God has condescended to the human and has carried it away
into the abyss of the Trinity.

The types of traditional holiness are characterized by the
heroic style of the desert, the monastery. By taking a certain
distance from the world, this holiness is stretched toward
heaven, vertically, like the spire of a cathedral. Nowadays,
the axis of holiness has moved, drawing nearer to the world.
In all appearances, its type is less striking; its achievement is
hidden from the eyes of the world, but it is the result of a
struggle that is no less real. Being faithful to the call of the
Lord, in the conditions of this world, makes grace penetrate
to its very root, where human life is lived.

The "little way" of St Theresa, that of the followers of
Charles de Foucauld, that of the Churches that are under
the sign of the Cross, but which pray and transform man by
their silence because they love him—this way is typical of the
modern response to the call of the Gospel. In the wake of
those who seize the Kingdom of God through the violence
of their loud humanism, the new holiness lays hold of it by
means of a certain "spiritual childhood," through integrity of
soul and the ascetic accomplishment of a nature put into the
services of God in all its fullness. More universally human,

closer to the realization of Christianity *in the world*, this new way nonetheless rejoins the essential values of all ages through interiorization.

It abandons the heights of mystical discourse to bring help to the world in distress; it bends over human misery, and goes down into the infernos of the modern world. The instinctive life, like the physiological, has no need to justify itself. Grace permeates all the levels of human life, and all of humanity is rehabilitated, restored to God in the one who gives himself fully to God. For a long time, the spirituality of the desert has remained in the margin of the ordinary life. The present-day world calls for a holiness that is capable of finding an answer to its problems, through a solution lived in the midst of the world.

Secularized eschatology deprives itself of the *eschaton,* the end, and dreams of a communion of saints without the Holy One, of a kingdom of God without God. When the servants of the Good become weak, the same task is taken over by forces of a different nature, preferring the antithetical sign, and confusion breaks out. The Gospel command to "seek first the Kingdom of God" (cf. Mt 6:33) becomes secularized and degenerates into the utopia of paradise on earth.

Nowadays, Christianity no longer is the active agent of history, but the spectator of events that escape its hold and run the risk of placing the Church in the margin of the world's destiny. Social and economic reforms and the liberation and emancipation of groups and social classes are affected by factors of this world that are removed from the Church.

At this hour, Christians everywhere live under the regime of a separation of Church and State. The Church can only adapt itself to this situation by keeping intact the universal and absolute character of its mission, inherent in its nature. Its theocratism, however, becomes more inward. It calls for the Church to be present everywhere as a *conscience* whose voice resounds unimpeded, addressing itself to freedom outside every secular imperative. If this voice loses its immediate pertinence because the means of the State are lacking, it gains moral power through the sovereign independence that its word acquires. In a climate of indifference or of open hostility, the Church, having lost all formal audience, can rely only on the faith of the people of God, untrammeled by compromise and conformity.

The victory gained earlier in the desert was more spectacular than the "triumph" of the empire of Constantine; plunging deep into deserted places, the monks left the empire that was protected all too well by the shadows of compromise. The desert, "the place of demons," is located nowadays in the heart of those who "live in the world without hope and without God" (Eph 2:12). The monks no longer have to leave the world; every believer can find his vocation under the completely new form of *interiorized monasticism*.

The theology of the last things requires that thought itself be lifted onto its own cross. There is no continuity between the cross and human philosophy: "We teach the things that no eye has seen and no ear has heard, things beyond the mind of man, all that God has prepared for those who love him" (cf. 1 Co 2:9). It encompasses all of Revelation, posits the mystery of eschatological man—*Filius Sapientiae* (the son of wisdom)—and leads to the magnificent definition of Christians everywhere, "all who have longed [for] His appearing" (2 Tm 4:8). For those who love the Parousia, the coming hour is the present hour.

The Gospel of John brings us an utterance of Christ that is perhaps the most serious one addressed to the Church: "He who receives any one whom I send receives me; and he who receives me receives Him who sent me" (13:20). If the world, man, our partner, receives a member of the Church, one of us, he is already inside the gradual movement of communion; he is no longer outside the sacred circle of the triune communion, of the Father's blessing. The destiny of the world depends on the resourceful attitude of the Church, on its skill at making itself welcome. Hell does not depend on God's anger; it depends perhaps on the cosmic charity of the saints: "To see our Lord in one's brother," "to always feel oneself hanging on the cross," "not to cease adding fire to fire, until death."

In the First Letter of John, the love of God is a beginning, preceding everything and transcending every response.

In its depth, love appears disinterested, like the servant's pure oblation, like the joy of the friend of the Bridegroom, a joy that exists by itself, like the air in sunlight, a preexistent joy for everyone. In Jn 14:28, Christ asks His disciples to be joyous with this immense joy, the reason of which transcends man, joy in the unique, objective existence of God. The salvation of the world proceeds from this limpid, pure joy.

Nonmonastic Celibacy

"There are varieties of gifts . . . there are varieties of service . . . there are varieties of working. . . . To each is given the manifestation of the Spirit for the common good. . . . All these are inspired by one and the same Spirit, who apportions to each one individually as he wills" (1 Co 12:4-11).

St Paul speaks of the gifts and the services one receives in view of a *diakonia* (ministry) for the common good. No one is excluded from the general appeal addressed to all, but as in a choir, one should discern one's own musical part, an entirely personal vocation, a unique destiny.

It is a decisive moment in a person's biography—in so far as it is a spiritual act and the taking of a position—when neither the monastic state nor marriage is found on the way. Turning a condition that is merely imposed by the circumstances of life into a destiny would be a disastrous error. The absence of something can never fill or form a being. And to expect nothing more from life would be to surrender to the most calamitous temptation. Positive waiting takes charge of the present without in the least prejudging the next day. To be positive and enriching, the true renunciation of a given situation (for instance, marriage) can only be a condition for the free and full acceptance of another (celibacy, for example), only the starting point of an actual vocation that will fill the existing present moment, always accepted and taken upon oneself, but never undergone.

*   *   *

This brings up the specific problem of the *vocation*. In its

immediate aspect, it is an inclination resulting from corre-
sponding attitudes, from natural gifts that are predisposed
toward a given type of life and activity. On the deeper level
and on the religious plane of faith, it is a more hidden, more
mysterious predisposition that carries the design of God for
a concrete human being. It is the essence of myself that God
proposes to me as the better part, the ideal part of myself
that I accept in advance and assume freely. It calls for a
totally open availability, which does not prejudge the following moment in the least.

Faith is an almost imperceptible, infinitely delicate prompt-
ing of grace that protects and safeguards the complete freedom that we have in pronouncing our fiat. We can only say
Yes because we can say No and build on a denial. The voice
of grace is never that of a tyrant; it is an invitation, a call
from the Friend. I accept it for today in the contours of my
present situation until the moment when I will *perhaps* see
more clearly. We should accept this vagueness of open, though
still undefined, horizons without obstructing them by bound-
aries arising from mere psychological factors, from a Freudian
necessity that controls the freedom of the spirit.

If the need arises, even a monk can break his vows. A
married man can become a monk. A single man can see opening before him one of the two paths, as he finds himself from
the perspective of celibacy in the world. For the time being
he accepts *this situation* cheerfully, with joy; he views it as a
task limited to today, as the present and the full value of his
life. The inevitable gropings that follow from this are accompanied by alternate successes and failures. However, it is
crucial to understand that it is never a question of a bleak,
imposed "duty," of a blind, relentless categorical imperative.
Possible pragmatic failures, discouragement, and momentary
bitterness do not in the least warrant a negation, an emptiness, a surrender. As one hand searches for another hand in
the dark, one should conform to grace, and wait with a smile
until such a material defeat is transformed into a spiritual
victory. The immediate finality, reached or not, is not at all
the absolute end of one's destiny.

A groping search quickly becomes a *directed* search when

it is passionate and sensitive to grace. This is never a mechanical interlocking, but rather the highest degree of correspondence between the call and the person. Little by little, the adumbrated value begins to come alive inside. I make it personal and give it a countenance that is mine. There is nothing external that can define me; by accepting *all* the conditions around me, I define them, my freedom—even when this entails suffering and the fire of purification, as it certainly does.

* * *

The empirical self is preoccupied only with itself and its blind desires; but the deeper, spiritual self, the one that assumes its destiny, runs ahead of the invitations, and hears and appropriates them. By responding to the call, or by accepting the present because of a lack of clarity, one finds oneself between specific present conditions and an inspiration. This may at any moment lead to an entirely new configuration; during this temporary pause between what is and will occur, I accept my vocation-destiny and somehow develop it from within. As an invitation to collaborate, the working of God embraces the working of man; the one is placed inside the other without ever forcing it. This is the profound dialectic, the perpetually virgin miracle of the human fiat, a dialectic that is not understood in terms of causality but in terms of creative participation. I am not the cause of my destiny, for it is a gift; but it lies within me to determine whether I am ruled by it or reject it or have dominion over it.

One should be informed and aware of the temptation to stubbornly multiply and magnify difficulties into the impossible. However, the unfeasible is the surest sign of an authentic vocation, since "the power of God is manifest in human weakness." Excessive worries and anxieties that lead to neuroses are an indication of an idolatry of one's own desires, of an exaggerated feeling of self-importance. There is a great difference between the call to the unknown and this totally unmotivated resolve that the empirical self creates without admitting it. The despair of an apparently failed life derives from the fact that one has assumed and decided beforehand that one will be a composer, a genius, an explorer, or a married man. Such an arbitrary resolution is a mortgage on the future; it does not take into account elements presently unknown but which in themselves are the best condition for an authentic destiny. The path that we guess and decide on in advance when we follow our passions and preferences, without screening them through an ascesis that reveals what is real, leads to the tragic dead ends of a ruined life.

Against all predetermined solutions one must discover the spiritual dimension of the free spaces in order to call forth creative reactions that transcend a given condition. All reduction of a destiny to an exterior determinism is illegitimate; one's vocation is found exactly on the crest between necessity and creative freedom, along the line of faith, which reveals the direction as its free and strong confession grows.

The one who is attentive awaits and already loves the event that is taking shape at the precise, mysterious junction where an unbeliever would see only nature and necessity. Ultimately, a vertical transcendence leaps up, even from a circle closed at the horizon.

When we think that we give up what we imagine to be ours, we only surrender that which restricts us. But this liberation occurs only at a time when the self ceases to take an interest in itself as an absolute end. We can add new ears to the sheaf of conditions, and then our whole, creative self shall bear fruit in every grain.

One's entire vocation is an option, an answer to a call that has been heard. It can simply be the present condition. It is never a voice that clarifies everything. The dimness inherent in faith never leaves us. There is one thing we can be sure of, that every vocation is always accompanied by a renunciation. One who is married renounces monastic heroism; a monk, the married life. The rich young man of the Gospel is not invited either to marry or to enter a monastery. He had to renounce his wealth, his "having," his *preferences,* in order to follow the Lord. Likewise, the "eunuchs" for the Kingdom—whatever meaning might be given to this expression—signal a deprivation, a renouncing, a sacrifice. However, in all the cases of deprivation Scripture speaks of, grace offers a gift; out of a negative renunciation it creates a positive vocation. To renounce one thing means to be totally consecrated to another that this very renunciation allows us to realize. It is not a mutilation at all, but a re-making of the "economy" of a being, put at the complete disposal of a new destiny already loved. All aridity of spirit results from sublimations that are badly assumed, from the forced maimings of a vocation that was poorly understood, from a disguised, paralyzing refusal. From these various modes of inauthenticity where life has no meaning, a passage to a world of true life opens up.

All men seek knowledge, power, joy. Only joy is sufficient unto itself. It comprises and surpasses everything, because it is the symphony of Meaning found, of the "one thing needful" about which the Gospel speaks.

* * *

The call to be celibate is infinitely greater than celibacy as such. It is not celibacy that is central, but a life that for the time brings celibacy with it. For a priest of the Roman Church, celibacy is only a *condition of his ministry* and presents no specifically monastic appeal. If Canon Law changes, the priest will be able to marry without betraying his vocation as priest, as is the case in the Eastern Church. Likewise, for an unmarried man celibacy is only a temporary or qualifying condition of the ministry of his royal priesthood, with a view to the Kingdom. If a monk is preoccupied "with the things of God," the unmarried man lives in "these things of God" which every human being sets up; his ministry is at the service of a neighbor. He moves in the second person, a *Thou* for the world in which he lives. This is the love-compassion that seeks neither reciprocity nor anything for itself, but gives of itself and descends into the inferno of a world agonizing in darkness. He does not choose, but bends over all suffering and encounters the other, the neighbor, who has abandoned God.

Such a life centered on the neighbor is a very concrete vocation, for it is a sign of the Kingdom, of its presence *in* the world. If salvation is beyond the world, it is in the world that it is offered. A demand coming from the world summons one to remain there as a witness to the Gospel. It is to such witnesses that the words of Augustine are applicable, "Give me someone who loves, and he will understand." It is a question here of cherishing one's destiny, of loving the cross formed by one's own "me." It is possible that the most ascetic act is not renunciation of self, but total self-acceptance. If I receive what befalls me as my own choice, everything becomes meaningful at that moment, profound, filled with a joyful and passionate interest. The human being is never alone; the hand of God is upon him. If he knows how to accept and feel it, his destiny is worked out, "oriented" toward the East. This is the experience of all the great spiritual masters.

*   *   *

For the woman who feels left out, who is disappointed by the expectation and the promises of her youth, *everything begins at the moment when everything seems closed and finished.* This is the profound meaning of the Grail legend.[13] A poor knight arrives when everything stands still, the old king is immobilized on his pallet, the springs have dried up, the birds no longer sing, and everything is held fast by the immobility of death. The knight asks a single question, the only true one, "Where is the Grail?" And then everything comes back to life, the old king leaves his sickbed, the springs run once more, and the birds sing again. This one question-answer is that of the fiat of our destiny. More than accepted or created, it transforms the given situation into spiritual gifts; the human being then lives his own miracle and lives in the miraculous. This is the precise meaning of the admirable passage in Isaiah: "Sing, O barren one, who did not bear; break forth into singing and cry aloud, you who have not been in travail! For the children of the desolate one will be more than the children of her that is married, says the Lord. . . . For your Maker is your husband . . ." (Is 54:1-5).

[13]*Perceval*, ed. Hucher; Jessie L. Weston, *From Ritual to Romance* (Cambridge, 1920).

The experience of life in Soviet Russia demonstrates the decisive role of woman in the renewal of religious life. At the moment when the Church became quiet because of the imposed reign of silence, the woman's kerygmatic activity, her true priesthood, rang out. She has fulfilled the mission of the apostles by building a world of faith in a world of anti-faith. Through her openness to the Spirit, she has "sensitized" souls to the Word. Without seeking anything, she has looked into her soul and has recognized herself in her vocation as the servant of God who awakens and sends out the friends of the Bridegroom.

In the ascesis of the great spiritual masters, humility means the art of finding oneself exactly at one's place. If in the world all desire the honors of the Bridegroom and the Mistress, the Gospel shows the true attitude of the handmaid of the Lord and of the Friend of the Bridegroom, and their joy is great for they hear the voice of the Lord.

* * *

The forms of social life undergo rapid and unforeseen changes; by contrast, the religious action of every believer possesses a great stability. He can become attentive to the designs of God in the prodigious progress of science and technology; he can bring together those who are lonely and create living communities of witnesses; he can kindle the spirit of adoration and make a prayer out of every work, even in the cemented heart of the most modern city. However, it is no longer possible to perform this ministry individually. The state of today's society demands deeds and measures that are the result of collective charity. It is collegially, on the part of men of prayer, that faith has the magnificent privilege of invoking the rights of God over the city of men. It is precisely here that the unmarried are the favorite agents, for they can dispense their available reserves of active charity without calculating.

If, as John Chrysostom maintains, marriage is "the image of heaven," celibacy is a more direct image of the Kingdom "where there is no marriage" and "where one is like the angels." The world to come will know neither the twin world of couples nor such a "man" as the man faced by such a "woman" as woman, but will know the unity of the masculine and the feminine in their totality, Adam-Eve restored to the spiritual dimension. It is therefore neither as a monk on the fringe of life nor as spouses who have partly withdrawn from it to build their unity but as anticipation of the future unity of the male and the female that the unmarried bring their total presence into the service of an effective friendship. Such a confraternity, wide as the world, assembling men and women, will bend *nuptially* over all human misery. ("Nuptially" here means uniting their spiritual gifts.)

An encounter may happen on this road, a pair may be formed through the will of God, *but in addition*. All exclusive and intentional search for such ties would warp the initial inspiration, the purity of the gift, through unavowed, but all the more neutralizing, conditions.

The transparency of the gift of self is decisive. Friendships, as deep as they are pure, may be started; in these, the soul finds its harmonious unfolding in a person-to-person relationship. Celibacy has not in the least prevented certain great Christian figures from displaying communion of soul, from developing a mystical friendship in an activity together —St Benedict and St Scholastica, St Francis and St Clare, St Francis of Sales and Jane Frances de Chantal, St John of the Cross and St Theresa, St John Chrysostom and Olympias the deaconess. Such friendships are not even contrary to the monastic state. They can produce a large offspring, spiritual children who follow their own vocation of witnessing.

The very special devotion of the great mystics toward the Theotokos emphasizes an important trait. Contrary to all morbid deviation, it draws purity from it, a chaste tenderness, the condition of being enamored with every creature. This is because the Virgin, in her motherly and consoling protection, is the strongest expression of the philanthropy of God. In this adage of the ascetics there is also a lesson that is no less instructive. "The hour that you are living, the person you are meeting, and the task that you are doing in this moment are the most important in your life." What we have immediately before us is the priestly oblation of self which in this moment triumphs over each separation, every loneliness, and every "death instinct." For the one who has fully taken up his vocation, the morrow becomes identical with the day of the Lord.

The magnificent words of St Gregory of Nyssa can be applied to every human condition; they unveil the miracle of a life joyfully received and given:

> We must fit together by a kind of necessary sequence even those statements concerning man that are opposed . . . so that the seeming contradictions are brought to one and the same end, *the power of God being capable of discovering a hope for what is beyond hope, and a way for what is inextricable.*[14]

---

[14]*De hominis opificio,* PG 44:128B.

4.

Love and the Sacrament of Love

The Harmonics of Love

To the question, "What *do* you do in life?" Oblomov, the
hero of the Russian Goncharov's novel, astonished and even
offended by such an inquiry, replies: "What? What am I
doing? Why, I am in love with Olga!" A striking confirmation, the content of which remains nonetheless inexpressible;
when dealing with first truths one may contrive, if necessary,
to explain the *how,* never the *why* or the *what.* Quite simply,
"They loved each other because all things desired that it be
so: the earth below, the sky above, the clouds and the trees"
(Pasternak, *Doctor Zhivago*); or again, "Because it was he,
because it was she" (*Tristan*).

None of the great thinkers or poets have ever found an
answer to the question, "What is love?" We can follow its
evolution but can say nothing of its birth. At the height of its
ascent, love becomes pure music and ceases to speak. If one
imprisons the light, it slips through the fingers. If a formula
of love were possible, one would have discovered the formula
of man himself. When all the arrows of reason are exhausted,
there remains the last one, that of myth, to speak to us of
love's irrational essence. Thus Ramuz writes in *Adam and
Eve,* "One and one cease to be two, and *remain one.*" They
do not become but remain one, which means that they rediscover and restore their initial mysterious unity.[1] Likewise,

---

[1]"The great miracle is that God has made two out of one and that these
two remain one," Jakob Boehme.

Shakespeare says in "The Phoenix and the Turtle," "So they loved, as love in twain/Had the essence but in one;/Two distincts, division none;/Number there in love was slain./ Either was the other's mine." "The beloved is inside me," Japanese poets say. The Kabbalah[2] sees in the beloved woman an apparition of the Shekinah, the Divine Presence. Dostoevsky perceives the same revelation and calls the beloved being "the living life" (*The Adolescent*). It is this power to make immortal that is affirmed by Gabriel Marcel: "To tell someone, 'I love you,' amounts to saying, 'You will never die.' "[3]

To have some idea about love, one should indeed move beyond love, to that depth of the soul where passion, safeguarding the intensity of its inner being, is freed from all carnal exaltation and becomes the unmoving center of a turning wheel. In transcending the sensual, love gives an unsuspected depth to the flesh. Clearsighted and prophetic, it is above all revelation. It makes one view the soul of the beloved in terms of radiance, and attains the level of knowledge that belongs only to the one who loves. In Hebrew the verb *yada* means both to know and to marry; loving, therefore, indicates complete knowledge, "Adam knew Eve." Behind all travesties, love contemplates the innocence that was at the beginning. Its miracle destroys remoteness, distance, solitude, and gives an inkling of what the mysterious unity of love can be, a heterogeneous identity of two subjects. In *The Fountain*, Charles Morgan states very well the final alternative of love: "Either you and I were by our discovery of each other made gods with power to create, in our relationship, a perdurable essence, higher than ourselves, independent of our delights, or we were animals caught in a trap. . . . Our love would create of itself a personality—a hypostasis—more beautiful and vital and lasting than ourselves, or it was a sterile pleasure . . ."[4]

By saying that "love is the fatherland of the soul," Gogol shows its ambiguity and places the same alternative before

[2]In Hebrew, Kabbalah means "oral tradition." Since the twelfth century it has been a collection of Jewish mystical doctrines. The most representative book is *Sefer Ha-Zohar,* "The Book of Splendor."
[3]*The Mystery of Being* II (Regnery, 1951), p. 171.
[4](New York: Alfred Knopf, 1932), p. 207-8.

us. A state of passion can remove all barriers. When it becomes completely despotic, love consumes and destroys; it changes into hatred and death (such is the destructive love of Versilov in Dostoevsky and the seduction of the woman "in love with the devil" in Gogol). However, the soul can also abide in the feminine-virginal and meet its Creator in the chaste newness of love.

While moving through all the dimensions of love, Durrell describes Eros as an awesome guide through the paths of suffering. Having deeply wounded-purified the human being, and after impressing the indelible stigmata on the chosen loved one (Clea's mutilated hand becomes like that of a new-born), Eros brings the soul to the summit of the purifying initiation and abandons it at the threshold of the palace where Art alone resides. Here love abdicates and decreases so that the other—Pure Art—may increase. The whole problem is to know what Art is . . .

Dostoevsky would have replied without hesitation that "the direct understanding of beauty is the Holy Spirit." As soon as one leaves the wake of the infernal ship and escapes the nets of the demonic fowler, at that moment, the day breaks over the cosmic Temple where the one artist, the Holy Spirit, resides.

The beloved being is not a god, but a royal gift, radiating the presence of the Giver. Dante states this in simple terms: She looked at God and I saw Him as He was reflected in her eyes, and the heaven was more blue, "To love what one will never see repeated": in this ever virginal newness, to love means to look together to the East. The darkest element changes into light; the dull coal becomes a sparkling diamond. The root buries itself in the dark soil, but the flower becomes light and triumphs over the darkness.

* * *

If no one has ever found a solution, if every age looks for one in its own way, it is because love is always a new subject. We may indicate its three harmonics: Greek, scriptural, and modern.[5]

[5]Cf. Jean Guitton, *L'amour humain* (Paris, 1948).

In Plato, love inaugurates the dialectic of transcendance. The winged souls mentioned in *Phaedrus* are born from amorous passion.

But the object of love fades away, and it is rapidly transcended toward the sublime and the intelligible, the essence of which is profoundly impersonal. Eros is a spirit (*daimon*), an "intermediary mediating between the mortal and the immortal," a powerful means, a spark triggering the ascent toward the purely spiritual, where the sage "will suddenly have revealed to him a beauty that neither comes into being nor passes away, neither waxes nor wanes."[6] This is the ascension toward the impersonal idea, with no dialogue, no reciprocity of love. The beauty of a particular outward form is a reflection and a reminiscence of the Beautiful in heaven. The pursuit of this Beauty consists in moving beyond the particular beloved, even in leaving him behind. This is the boundary of love in Plato. Nonetheless, it is already a pre-ascesis that withdraws from the sensual, from the deception of the senses.

Denis de Rougemont mythanalyzes modern love, love as passion, and traces its origin to the myths of Tristan and Isolde, and that of Don Juan. Passion is consummated in great sorrow, through excessive suffering, and leads to a welcome death in the name of the mystique of night. At the other extreme, Don Juan is the one who cheats; he loves only his love and violates the truth of beings. He tastes women as one tastes fruit, without either giving or taking away the soul. In his own way Don Juan might possibly be Neoplatonic. He loves no woman in particular; he seeks "the feminine" of which every woman is but an imperfect reflection. In the end, he himself ceases to be a concrete individual and he becomes "a man without a name," insubstantial (Tirso de Molina).

The action of these myths is projected into the real life of couples, and triggers crises. If asceticism does not permeate eternal duration, duration begets a fearful boredom. The intensity of Tristan, not contained by time, endeavors to escape beyond time. The always new excitement of Don Juan is

<hr>

[6]*The Symposium* 202-211, trans. Walter Hamilton (New York, 1951), p. 93.

limited to just the first mornings of love and denies tomorrow, the duration. These are two ways of loving, both of which destroy the loved one. Passionate "angelism" and the Tristan death-wish destroy the historic aspect of the beloved; they change into the Don Juan subversion which destroys the beloved's eternal dimension. In another connection, troubadour poetry idealizes love. But, unstable on account of its romanticism, thirsty yet Platonizing, powerless to remain on the summits of ascetic purity, its love fails in the face of the sarcasm of an easy libertinism, and it ends by praising death.

In Kierkegaard's romanticism, woman, "the gateway to heaven," becomes pure idea: "It is woman's misfortune to represent everything in the moment, and to represent nothing more in the next moment, without ever truly knowing what she properly signifies as woman." When man is no longer in need of inspiration, or when he feels threatened by duration, the woman no longer has any firmness or value in herself; she is not even a human subject, a person, but at the most a relative being, a poetic form of absence.

Marx and Freud do their utmost to tear away the romantic masks in order to discover the brutal reality of secret desires in the place of love, an exploitation of the one by the other. The unveiled humans are degraded to males and females. A misunderstood ascesis led Nietzsche to write, "Christianity gave Eros poison to drink; he did not die of it but degenerated into vice." When the Gospel is not accepted in its totality, the conflict between the spirit and the senses creates at once a profound lack of balance. Every solution that seeks to "unsex" the human being is an attempt on the creative will of God. To mortify Eros by mortifying the flesh is to dangerously desiccate the human being; it is to move from a scorn of the disturbing element to hatred of it.

"Man can be imagined without woman . . ."; he makes history without viewing it through the eye of the revelation of Scripture. However, St Paul says: "In the Lord woman is not independent of man or man of woman" (1 Co 11:11).

The Song of Songs, the most sublime of all poems, praises love and the sacred dyad of the nuptial union.[7] As a wedding

[7]Historians surmise that the Song was sung during the Jewish marriage

song, it shows the betrothed searching for one another, but its real subject is neither the bucolic shepherd nor the beautiful Shulamite, but Love itself.[8] The Song was written because of the theme expressed in the closing lines: "Set me as a seal upon your heart, as a seal upon your arm; for love is strong as death. . . . *Its flashes are flashes of fire, a most vehement flame"* (Sg 8:6). As an image of the love of the betrothed, it is also a figure of the nuptial love between God and the human soul. The essential revelation of the Song is that human love has its source in God and is kindled by the tongues of the devouring fire of Jahweh, a nuptial Pentecost.

In his book, *The Jasmine of the Faithful of Love,* the great Persian mystic Ruzbehan Bagli of Shiraz views lived human love as a necessary initiation into the love of God. This is not the monastic conversion of Eros, but its transfiguration. In every beloved there is an encounter with the one and only Beloved, just as in every divine name the totality of Names is found again, due to the sympathetic union (*unio sympathetica*). Beauty is seen as a manifestation of the sacred (*hierophany*), an apparition of the divine (*theophany*), only if the love of God is lived in human love, the element to be transfigured and transmuted. Human love seems propaedeutic to divine love.[9]

The Song brings together what Plato—and with him all the romantic or ascetic trends—dissociates. In Biblical anthropology, the love between a man and a woman has its origin in the love of God, and leads to God. The poetic form used by the Semitic genius praises the charms of beauty and humanizes love, but also raises it to the level of the divine. The Song transfigures passing desires into the unique thirst for the Absolute. In this manner, Scripture does away with every disembodied idealization and invites us to come to terms with the human being in its totality, baptized and destined for the Resurrection.

---

ceremony. It recapitulates and enlarges upon the first utterance of human love, "This at last is flesh from my flesh" (Gn 2:22).

[8] Cf. Sergius Bulgakov, *Le Paraclet* (Paris: Aubier), p. 314.

[9] See Henry Corbin, *L'imagination créatrice dans le soufisme d'Ibn'Arabi.*

The Prophetic Revelations and the Eternal Present

In the violent, overpowering attraction of lovers, Eros recognizes the beloved object of its dreams. We may speak of a certain *anamnesis* (remembrance), a mysterious reminiscence found in each true love. Every man carries within himself his own Eve, and lives in the expectation of her possible Parousia. This presentiment gives beauty and purity to the poetic dreams of adolescence. An attentive man may have a certain inkling of being born for true love, if such is his destiny: "she was destined for you from eternity" (Tb 6:17), the angel Raphael tells Tobias. The presence of God is no stranger to the attraction lovers feel for one another, and their encounter is never fortuitous. The beloved countenance was already known; it preexisted before it was encountered and recognized.

On the road to Emmaus, Christ makes Himself known to the disciples at the moment of the breaking of bread. This moment also exists in love; it is a very pure instant when the lovers taste the "bread of angels" and recognize one another in a direct, sudden revelation. As lightning pierces the darkness, so lovers behold one another: "he sees himself in the beloved as in a mirror" and "as in water face answers to face, so the heart of man to man."[10]

Prophetic insight contemplates the "beauty of the hidden man of the heart"; it understands the icon that is shining through, the thought of God concerning the beloved. Love wells up at the precise moment when "some hidden hand unveils to him the loveliness that others cannot understand."[11] What is common and lacks the mysterious for the noninitiated suddenly becomes unique and mysterious. It is said that love is blind, and yet it makes one see. The revelation is trans-subjective but not illusive, for it depends on the image of God. The iconographic concept acquaints and accustoms one to see the image of eternity. It is in this sense that St John Chrysostom affirms that "nuptial love is the strongest love";

10Proverbs 27:19.
11Coventry Patmore, *The Angel in the House* (Boston, 1960), p. 54.

like faith it is able to see what is hidden to others. Love breaks through hidden depths, its arrival fulfills and perfects, but it does not exhaust the mystery.

One is loved for what one is, which allows one to accept oneself and to receive one's own being as a gift. An average person develops into a genius of love. A song that welled up from his roots can fill the universe and raise it to a level hitherto unknown.

However, this "birth into beauty" brings with it a purifying fire and imposes an asceticism. The banquet of love does not last. The face of the beloved is shown, only to disappear again. This is because it is not only given; it must also be created. It charms the human being and then, concealing itself, it leaves a deep nostalgia in the heart, a burning desire for its presence.

The day-to-day profanes the sacred, and everything conspires tirelessly to convince man that love does not keep its promises, does not overcome all-powerful *duration*. Life is nothing but wear and tear, an eternal dying that beclouds the radiant face of the Shulamite who has appeared for a fleeting moment. Nothing withstands the melancholy grip of time. It distorts the features of the beloved; it sorely tries the newness of the first morning and the initial inspiration. It is in the fearsome struggle against duration and murderous repetitions that the human being appears most vulnerable. The prosaic in life brings him down to the infernal element of boredom. The soul is alarmed by its stumbling and its inevitable failures; the vision fades away and it seems that nothing is left but conflicts and contradictions.

Kierkegaard loves Regina Olsen; he loves the young girl in her, the young girl in general. In her, he seeks what is beyond her. To transform the young girl into a woman would for him be a work of destruction. His way is that of a poet, of an ascetic who begets minds but does not get married. To be married is to confront a terrifying danger: getting settled in life, dozing off into the sleep of death. This is what Victor Eremita (this name means "victory of the hermit") expresses in *The Banquet* or *In Vino Veritas*:

In Tieck's romantic dramas one sometimes runs across
a character who once was a king in Mesopotamia and
is now a greengrocer in Copenhagen . . . The girl
Juliana, once an empress in love's far-reaching realm,
is now Madame Petersen at the corner of Bathhouse
Street . . .

But here is the most alarming passage of all:

Many a genius became a genius through a girl, many
a hero became a hero through a girl, many a poet
became a poet through a girl, many a saint became a
saint through a girl; but who has become a genius,
a poet, a hero, or a saint through the influence of his
wife? Through her he became only a Privy Councillor,
a general, a father. There is a deplorable seriousness:
to get married, to have children, to have gout, to pass
the theological examination, to become a deputy . . .[12]

A cruel mirror of human conditions into which spouses would
do well to look ceaselessly at themselves. Life gives the alternative to death: to die in the Resurrection, or else to anticipate
Hell.

The case of Kierkegaard—a modern replica of that other
Dane, young prince Hamlet—is typical of the radicalism of
poetic romanticism, which is not exactly the evangelical absolute of the Incarnation. For Kierkegaard, Regina was the *Virgo
mater* inspiring his work. He remains the poet, and "stares
with the inner sadness of Merman the seducer who from the
bottom of the sea contemplates Agnete playing and singing
on the shore." His entire work is a homage to the one chosen
by his imagination; it becomes a dialogue totally removed
from the concrete human being whose destiny it does not
share. "Had I had faith," he says, "I should have remained
with Regina."[13] He tastes "the young girl" like an abstract

12*Stages on Life's Way*, trans. Walter Lowrie (Princeton University Press,
1945), p. 69-70.
13*The Journals of Kierkegaard*, ed. Alexander Dru (New York, 1959),
p. 86.

philosopher: she is neither accepted nor known, and does not receive the poet's soul in exchange. The sword of King Mark separates the two and turns them into categories of ideality: "The philosopher shudders mortally at *marriage*, . . . as a fatal hindrance on the way to the *optimum*. Up to the present what great philosophers have been married? A married philosopher belongs to *comedy*, that is my rule," affirms Nietzsche.[14]

Kierkegaard's religious attitude sheds some light: he remains *before* God but not *in* God. The element of transfiguration, the miracle of the metamorphosis of Cana, is tragically absent in him. He is crushed by the weight of sin, haunted by the thought of damnation. No refreshing breath of grace ever runs through the melancholic and ironic pages of his books, his life.

What is "unique" in love is never what is "general." Love is not a psychological fact within the immediate reach of human nature; it requires the mediation of grace. This is why marriage is not grounded in either the moral or the aesthetic, but in the religious. Through the grace of the sacrament, failures are never mortal wounds, nor are imperfections condemned without recourse. What the monks attain *directly*, the spouses work out *indirectly*, and their *means* is the sacramental sphere of grace. The one through the other they look at Christ, and it is "the Other," His love, that is the gift of grace. The young girl, then, remains eternally present in the woman, "You have kept the good wine until now," "a present" that is always virginal, saturated with the eternal. This is why Coventry Patmore sings of the "fruition of eternal freshness."

If one were to stand outside of the Incarnation, the infinite, qualitative, unbridgeable distance between man and God, His absolute otherness, it would make love unhappy and all communion, even communication, indirect and veiled. Projected into the relationships of the betrothed, the fundamental otherness of the other makes love especially unhappy and impossible. Matrimony is forbidden to the one who be-

[14]*The Genealogy of Morals: A Polemic*, trans. Horace B. Samuel (New York, 1964), p. 135.

comes productive only by keeping a negative relationship with the young girl, one made up of distance and, ultimately, absence (as in the case of Kierkegaard).

Without an obstacle no passion lasts. In marriage, the obstacle becomes greatly interiorized. The whole fascinating mystery of love lies in the spiritual conquest of the other, of the inaccessible. This makes of the beloved otherness the matter of the sacrament: the aim of love is that two become one (*finis amoris ut duo unum fiant*). A stranger becomes more intimate to me, more inward than my own soul. From this perspective, nuptial chastity for the man means that there is but one being in the world, that all femininity resides in her.

Under Emperor Maximian, a young Roman officer named Hadrian suffers heroic martyrdom, supported and strengthened until the moment of his death by Natalia, his young wife, who speaks only these words: "Blessed are you, my master, light of my life, for having been admitted to the number of the saints."

Arrayed in the everyday, the young girl in Natalia reaches the womanly maturity of an ear of wheat ripened in the sun. Entering upon sainthood, united to her husband in her oblation to the Lord, in his service until martyrdom, she is the "smile of God," the "tenderness of the Father."

The Image of God

There is but one suffering: to be alone. A one-personed God would not be love. God is Trinity, one and at the same time three. The human being, as a closed monad, would not be His image. The Biblical account calls woman a "helper meet for man," more precisely, a "face-to-face." Scripture does not state that it is not good "to work alone" but "to *be* alone," and thus the woman will "be with him." "One toward the other" forms their co-being; and thus it is from the beginning, *in principio*, that the human being has been a nuptial being, "And [He] named them Man when they were created" (Gn 5:2). "While speaking of two, God speaks of one," John Chrysostom observes.[15]

It is to their reciprocity, to their dyad of an ecclesial nature, that God addresses Himself when He uses both the singular and the plural forms of "you," without ever separating them. But an element alien to man, the demonic, implants a distance into their relationships and then, throughout history, the one will not stop saying to the other: "Where are you—*Ayekkah?* In what condition are you?" This ontological perversion is recorded in the words God addresses for the first time to each one separately: "To the woman He said . . ." and, "To Adam He said . . ." (Gn 3:16-17). This event proves that the differentiation between masculine and feminine is above all spiritual.

Indeed, the creation of Adam has been from the first the creation of the totality of man; in Hebrew, the word Adam-man is a collective term. The Book of Genesis says literally: "Let us make man [*ha adam,* in the singular] and let them [in the plural] have dominion. And God created man [in the singular] and He created them man-male and man-female [the plural refers to the singular, man]." "Man" transcends the male-female distinction, because the latter is initially not the separation of two individuals that are henceforth isolated from one another. On the contrary, we can state that these two aspects of man are at this point inseparable in the mind of God, and that a human being, taken in isolation and viewed by himself, is not fully human. In being removed from its complement there is, so to speak, only half a man.

God caused a deep sleep (*tardemah*) to fall upon the man. Here the Septuagint speaks of ecstasy. It is a question of a very special torpor, of the "suspension of the senses" announcing an event.[16] The birth of Eve projects into existence what was moving already inside the being. Adam has always been Adam-Eve. The advent of Eve is the great myth of *the nuptial consubstantiality of man and woman:* "She shall be called woman [*isha*], because she was taken out of man [*ish*]."

15*In Epist. ad Ephesios Homilia* XX, PG 62:135.
16Cf. Genesis 5:1-12. The deep sleep "fell upon Abraham."

Jerome translates this into Latin as *virago* and *vir*. The one from the other—they shall be one flesh, a single being: "my beloved is mine, and I am his" (Sg 2:16).

This archetypal order of creation is integrated into the order of grace at the wedding of Cana. The base of ancient wedding cups represented Christ holding two crowns above the spouses, the divine principle of the reintegration of the initial order. St John Chrysostom states this precisely: "The qualities of love are such that the beloved and the lover no longer form two beings, but one . . . They are not only brought together, but 'are one,'[17] which means man-woman, one 'adam' in the Biblical sense,[18] for 'love transmutes the very nature of things.' "[19] In a commentary on Genesis, St Cyril of Alexandria adds, "God created co-being."

This patristic concept is fundamental to the East and inspires all its canonical texts. Marriage is defined as "the unity of two persons in one being, a single substance" or "the union in one body and one soul, but in two persons." The definition is important; the nuptial "I" does not abolish the persons but is in the image of the Trinity. The union of the Three Persons in one nature forms a single Subject: God, one and at the same time triune. Likewise, the nuptial union of two persons forms a dyad-monad, at the same time two and one, united in a third person, God. "God made the woman together with the man, not only that thus the mystery of God's sole government might be exhibited, but also that this mutual affection might be greater."[20] It is therefore nuptial man who is in the image of the triune God, and the dogma of the Trinity is his divine archetype, the icon of the nuptial community.

In the priestly prayer of Christ we hear, "I have *glorified* them . . . that they may be one in us as we are one." The Service of Crowning of marriage announces that the spouses are "crowned with glory." The glory signifies the manifesta-

---

[17]*In Epist. I ad Cor. Homilia* XXXIII, PG 61:280; *In Epist. ad Coloss. cap. IV, Homilia* XII, PG 62:387.

[18]*In Epist. I ad Cor. Homil.* XXXIV, PG 61:289.

[19]*In Epist. I ad Cor. Homilia* XXXII, PG 61:273.

[20]Theophilus of Antioch, *To Autolycus* II. 28, trans. *The Ante-Nicene Fathers*, vol. II, p. 105.

tion of the Holy Spirit. This gift of the Spirit at Pentecost, His charism of unity, can be obtained only in the Church: "from [Christ] the whole body, joined and knit together by every joint with which it is supplied, when each part is working properly, makes bodily growth and upbuilds itself in love" (Eph 4:16). The living community of the Church results from the "bonds," the special forms of love. Alongside the monastic and the parish community another type of these forms-bonds is found, the nuptial love-community. Marriage forms an ecclesial dyad, constitutes a "domestic church," according to St Paul and St John Chrysostom.

"When husband and wife are united in marriage, they are no longer seen as something earthly, but as the image of God Himself." These words of St John Chrysostom allow us to see in marriage a living icon of God, a "theophany." Clement of Alexandria has a far-reaching concept: "But who are the two or three gathered in the name of Christ in the midst of whom the Lord is? Does He not by the two mean husband and wife?"[21] He nonetheless propounds one condition: "The prize in the contest of men is shown by him who has *trained* himself by the discharge of the duties of marriage; by him, I say, who in the midst of his solicitude for his family shows himself *inseparable from the love of God*."[22] "The state of marriage is holy"[23] because it anticipates the Kingdom and already constitutes a "little kingdom" (*micrabasileia*), its prophetic image. Each destiny crosses the critical point of its Eros, laden with deadly poisons but also with revelations from heaven, to catch sight of the transfigured Eros of the Kingdom where "men and women do not marry" and "are like the angels in heaven." These words signify not beings or isolated couples, but the nuptial harmony of the Masculine and the Feminine, the two dimensions of the one Pleroma in Christ. Alpha joins Omega. According to St Asteria, Adam's first words, "flesh of my flesh," were a declaration of the masculine with regard to the feminine precisely in their totality.[24]

[21]*Stromateis* III.10.68, PG 8:1169, trans. E. L. Oulton, *Alexandrian Christianity* (Philadelphia, 1954), p .71.
[22]*Stromateis* VII.12.70, PG 9:497, *ibid.*, p. 138.
[23]*Strom.* III. 12.84, PG 8:1185, *ibid.*, p. 80.
[24]PG 40; 228.

The Proper Aim of Marriage

The modern Western distinction between the objective aim (procreation) and the subjective aim (the nuptial community) is inadequate; it does not take account of the basic hierarchy. The texts of the Orthodox Church,[25] when they are not showing the influence of Western handbooks,[26] are unanimous in placing the aim of nuptial life in the spouses themselves. In his Dogmatic Theology, Metropolitan Macarius gives this definition, the most recent, one which is very clear and explicit, and says nothing about procreation: "Marriage is a sacred rite. The spouses promise reciprocal fidelity before the Church; the grace of God is bestowed through the blessing of the minister of the Church. It sanctifies their union and confers the dignity of representing the spiritual union of Christ and the Church."

The light that was at the beginning has been dispelled through the Fall. St Paul, while speaking of adultery, says "one body" (1 Co 6:16) instead of "one flesh," a complex term, thereby rendering the spiritual isolation, the frustrated communion, more incisive. Origen[27] draws attention to the first chapter in Genesis where mention is made of the male and the female; their natural union places man in the species, subjecting him to the commandment given to the animal kingdom: "Be fruitful and multiply." Man survives in his progeny, and through feverish fecundity he hastens to find in it an assurance of his survival. Only the Gospel makes us

[25]The *Nomocanon in XIV Titles; Procheiros Nomos* (title IV, chap. 1; *Basilica* 28.4; the commentaries of Balsamon; the *Syntagma* of Blastares; the *Hexabiblos* of Harmenopoulus; the *Pedalion;* the *Orthodox Confession* by Peter Moghila, question 115; the *Ecloga* of 740. The greater number of texts refer to the definition of marriage given by Modestinus, a Roman jurisprudent: *"Nuptiae sunt conjunctio maris et feminae et consortium omnis vitae, divini et humani juris communicatio,"* "union and community of life," without any mention of procreation. *Digesta* XXIII. 2.1. Quoted by S. Troitsky, *The Christian Philosophy of Marriage* (in Russian), p. 19.

[26]Chapter 50 of the *Kormchaia Kniga* (by Patriarch Joseph and Patriarch Nikon) is a seventeenth century translation of the Roman Catechism of 1561; certain passages of the Catechism by Metropolitan Philaret follow Bellarmine.

[27]*Comment. in Mattheum, tomus* XIV, *Scholia,* PG 13:1229.

understand that it is not in the species but in Christ that man is eternal, that he strips off the old man and "is renewed in the image of the One who has created him." Marriage grafts man into this renewal. The account of the institution of marriage, found in the second chapter of Genesis, speaks of "one flesh" without mentioning procreation at all. The creation of the woman is an answer to the statement, "It is not good for man to be alone." The nuptial community constitutes the person, for it is the "man-woman" that is in the image of God. All the New Testament passages dealing with marriage follow the same order and do not mention offspring (Mt 19; Mk 10; Eph 5). The coming of man completes the gradual creation of the world. Man humanizes the world and gives it a human and spiritual meaning. It is in man that the sexual differentiation finds its meaning and its proper value, independently of the species.

The economy of the Law ordained procreation to perpetuate the race, for the increase of the chosen people in view of the birth of the Messiah. In the economy of grace, however, the birth of the elect derives from the preaching of faith. The side from which the woman was taken no longer has this utilitarian role assigned to it by sociology. Nowadays the Arabs say, "he is my side," which signifies, "inseparable companion."

In the fourth century, St John Chrysostom further declares: "There are two reasons for which marriage was instituted . . . to bring man to be content with one woman and to have children, but it is the first reason that is the most important. As for procreation, it is not required absolutely by marriage . . . The proof of this lies in the numerous marriages that cannot have children. This is why the first reason of marriage is to order sexual life, especially now that the human race has filled the entire earth."[28]

In the image of the creative love of God, human love strives to "design" an object on which to pour itself. In itself, the existence of the world adds nothing to the fullness of God; nonetheless, it is this plenitude that confers on Him His quality as God. God is fullness, not for Himself, but for His

---

[28]*Peri gamou, On Marriage.*

creation. Likewise, the nuptial union in itself is plenitude.[29] It can, however, also acquire a new qualification out of its own superabundance: fatherhood or motherhood. The child born of this nuptial community prolongs it and reaffirms the already perfectly realized unity. Love contemplates its reflection in the world and begets the child. "When she has given birth to the child, the woman forgets her suffering in her joy that a man has been born into the world"; a new face is called to become an icon of God.

Motherhood is a special form of the feminine *kenosis* (emptying). The mother gives herself to the child, dies in part for it, follows the love of God that humbles itself, and in a certain sense repeats the utterance of John the Baptist, "He must grow greater, I must grow smaller." The sacrifice of the mother includes the sword of which Simeon speaks. In this sacrifice, every mother bends over the crucified Christ.

The veneration of the Virgin-Mother brings out the vocation of every woman, her charism of protecting and of nurturing. There is an ever growing number of beings in the world who live like those who are abandoned by God. Their existence is a call to every Christian household to express its nuptial priesthood, its true nature, as a "domestic Church" that receives only to give and thereby reveals itself as a force of compassion and help to return prodigal children to their Father.[30]

The Domestic Church

Clement of Alexandria[31] calls marriage the "House of God," and applies to it the words about the presence of the Lord, "I am in the midst of them" (Mt 18:20). According to St Ignatius of Antioch, then, "Where Jesus Christ is, there is the universal Church," which enables us to clearly see the

---

[29]St Basil observes that children add to the fullness of the nuptial union; they are *epakolouthema*, an "appendix," a possible but not indispensable result. *Liber de virginitate*, PG 30:745.

[30]On the subject of abandoned children, see Mad. Tasset-Nissole, *Le massacre des innocents.*

[31]*Stromatum liber* III, PG 8:1169.

ecclesial nature of the nuptial community. It is not by mere chance either that St Paul puts his magistral teaching on marriage in the context of his Letter on the Church, Ephesians. He speaks of the "domestic Church," *he kat' oikon ekklesia* (Rm 16:5). There is more here than a simple analogy. Biblical symbolism depends on a very intimate correspondence between the various levels, showing them as different expressions of a single Reality.

According to the Fourth Gospel (2:1-11), the first miracle of Christ takes places at the wedding at Cana. Through its very matter—water and wine—it serves as a prelude to Calvary and already announces the birth of the Church on the Cross, "out of the pierced side came blood and water." The symbolism brings together and links the place of the miracle, the wedding, to the eucharistic reality of the Church.

The presence of Christ bestows a sacramental gift upon the betrothed. It is of this that St Paul speaks when he states that "everyone has received his special gift from God." Through its action, the water of the natural passions is changed into "the fruit of the vine," the noble wine that signifies the transmutation into "the new love," a charismatic love springing forth to the Kingdom.

This is why the Theotokos, like a guardian angel, bends over the world in distress: "They have no more wine," she says. The Virgin means to say that the chastity of old, considered the integrity of being, has ceased. Nothing is left but the impasse of masculinity and femininity. The jars destined for the "ablutions among the Jews" are hardly sufficient; but "ancient forms have passed away"; the purification of the ablutions becomes baptism, "the bath of eternity," in order to grant access to the Eucharistic Banquet of the one and only Bridegroom.

The intercession of the Virgin hastens the arrival: "Do whatever He tells you." "People generally serve the best wine first and keep the cheaper sort"; the good wine of the betrothal is but a fleeting promise and is rapidly exhausted; the nuptial cup dries up—such is the order of nature. At Cana this order is reversed: "You have kept the best wine till now." This "now" is the moment of Christ; it knows no passing. The more the spouses are united in Christ the more their common cup, the measure of their life, is filled with the wine of Cana and becomes miraculous.

At Cana, Christ "manifested His glory" within the confines of a "household Church" (*ecclesia domestica*). In fact, this wedding is the wedding of the spouses to Christ. It is He who presides at the wedding of Cana and, according to the Fathers, at every Christian wedding. It is He who is the one and only Bridegroom whose voice the friend hears and in which he rejoices. This dimension of the mystical betrothal of the soul to Christ, of which marriage is the direct figure, is that of every soul and that of the Church-Bride.

In its full measure, all grace comes at the end of a sacrifice. The spouses themselves receive it from the moment they undertake to present themselves before the Father in heaven in their dignity as priests, and to offer to Him the sacrifice in Christ, the "reasonable gift," the oblation of their entire nuptial life. The grace of the priestly ministry of the husband and the grace of the priestly motherhood of the wife form and mold the nuptial being in the image of the Church.

By loving each other the spouses love God. Every moment of their life rises up like a royal doxology, like an unending liturgical chant. St John Chrysostom brings forward this magnificent conclusion: "Marriage is a mysterious icon of the Church."[32]

The Sacraments

Nicholas Cabasilas, the great liturgist of the fourteenth century, defines the sacraments in this way: "They are the path which Christ has made for us, the door He has opened. . . . It is by passing again on this path and through this door that He returns to the world."[33] Indeed, after the Ascension, Christ returns in the sacramental economy of the Holy Spirit. This economy continues its historical visibility and replaces the miracles at the time of the Incarnation.

[32]*In Epist. ad Coloss. cap.* IV, *Homilia* XII, PG 62:387.
[33]Nicholas Cabasilas, *The Life in Christ,* trans. Carmino J. deCatanzaro (New York: St Vladimir's Seminary Press, 1974), cf. p. 66.

The classical definition states that "the sacrament is a holy action through which the invisible grace of God is given to the believer under the visible sign."[34] They are not only signs that confirm the promises of God, neither are they means to invigorate faith and trust; they do not merely give, but *contain,* grace and are *channels;* they are at the same time the instruments of salvation and salvation itself, as is the Church.

The union of the visible and the invisible is inherent in the nature of the Church. As an ongoing Pentecost, the Church pours forth the superabundance of grace through every form of her life. But the institution of the sacraments (its *licit* side, the canonical correctness, its *valid* side and its *efficacious* side of sanctifying grace) establishes a structure that sets limits to all disordered, sectarian "Pentecostalism" and at the same time gives to all and everyone the unshakable, objective, universal foundation of the life of grace. The Spirit blows wherever it pleases, but in the sacraments, when the institutional conditions that are required by the Church are present and by virtue of the promise of Christ, the gifts of the Holy Spirit, the "events," are certainly given and the Church attests to this. Thus each sacrament calls, above all, upon the will of God that this act take place; then comes the act itself, the sacrament, and, in the third place, the testimony of its reception by the Church confirms the gift that has been given and received. In ancient practice, the *axios* (showing of agreement) or the *amen* by the people accompanied and sealed every sacramental act. In short, all the sacraments led to the Eucharist which, through its own fullness, completed the testimony of the Church. Such a *consensus* of catholicity is an inner reality of the Church. A sacrament is always an event *in* the Church, *through* the Church, and *for* the Church. It excludes everything that isolates ecclesial resonance. And thus for the sacrament of marriage, the husband and wife enter upon the eucharistic *synaxis*[35] in their new married life. The integration with the Eucharist testifies to the descent of the Spirit and to the gift received. This is why every

---

[34]*The Orthodox Confession,* Part I.
[35]The gathering of the faithful to celebrate the Eucharist.

sacrament has always been an organic part of the eucharistic Liturgy.

The world is lost in darkness, but the darkness can be seen only because it is pierced by shafts of the light that "enlightens every man that comes into the world." "The gates of Hell can never hold out against the Church," for until the end of the world, the sacraments, those arrows of fire, announce the saving power of grace and trace a dazzling way to the Kingdom.

For a long time the sacrament has ceased to be, for the majority, the mystery to which the entire heavenly world is invited each time it is performed. It has become nothing but a "practice," a "religious duty," a form like any other that the majority certainly wishes to make as hollow as any other of its social symbols. This "form," however, is completely filled with the presence of God, the vivid and fearful realism of the words of Scripture reminds us: "Take off your shoes, for this is holy ground." The Spirit makes the Church the place and the reason for being of the world. It pushes its walls back to the confines of the universe. It is in the Church that the flowers open up and the grass grows, that man is born, loves, dies, and rises again.

The matter of the sacrament is not only a "visible sign," but the natural substratum that is changed into the place where the energies of God are present. In the sacrament of marriage, the matter is the *love* of man and woman. According to Justinian, "Marriage is effected through pure love" (*Novella* 74, ch. 1) ; for St John Chrysostom it is love that unites the lovers and joins them to God.[36] Through the "Edenic grace" of the sacrament, love is transmuted into charismatic communion. The Letter to the Ephesians shows it as essentially a miniature of the nuptial love of Christ for the Church.

The Paradisiac Institution

That marriage was instituted in Paradise is a very solid, ancient tradition. While speaking of marriage, Christ refers

[36]*In Epist. ad Ephes. cap. V. Homilia* **XX**, PG 62:141.

to the Old Testament, "Have you not read?" (Mt 19:4; Mk
10:2-12). St Paul does likewise (Eph 5:31). Clement of
Alexandria states very clearly that "the Son only confirms what
the Father has instituted."[37] In the creation of man, Clement
saw the sacrament of baptism,[38] and in the loving communion
of the first couple, the divine institution of the sacrament of
marriage. He even speaks of the paradisiacal grace of marriage, *tes tou gamos charitos*.[39] Through this grace the Christian marriage receives something of the nuptial state before
the Fall.

Clement even says much more: "God created man male
and female. The male is Christ, the female is the Church."[40]
The love of Christ for the Church becomes the archetype of
marriage, and in this wise it exists before the couple, for
Adam is created in the image of Christ and Eve in the image
of the Church. We now understand why the first couple and
all couples are viewed in reference to this single image. St
Paul has formulated what is essential: "This mystery is a
profound one, and I am saying that it refers to Christ and the
Church" (Eph 5:32). Mystery, *mysterion*, has the meaning
here of an inexhaustibly rich content that one will enjoy for
all eternity. In the text of Genesis, St Paul sees a prophetic
prefiguration, its hidden meaning now made clear. Thus,
marriage goes back to before the Fall; as archetype of the
nuptial relations it explains the name of Israel and that of
the Church, the Bride of Jahweh. Neither the Fall nor time
have touched its sacred reality. The Orthodox Ritual specifies:
"Neither original sin nor the flood has in the least damaged
the sacredness of the nuptial union." St Ephrem of Syria adds,
"From Adam until Christ, authentic love was the perfect sacrament."[41] Rabbinical wisdom viewed married love as the only
channel of grace, even for pagans.[42] St Augustine teaches the
same: "At Cana, Christ confirms what He instituted in Para-

[37]*Stromatum liber* III, PG 8:1184.
[38]*Op. cit.*, III. 17, PG 8:1205.
[39]*Ibid.*, 14, PG 8:1196.
[40]*II ad Corinth.* 14.
[41]*In Ephesios* 5. 32.
[42]*Zohar*, I.

dise."[43] St John Chrysostom writes: "Christ has brought a gift, and through the gift He has honored the cause."[44] In his letter addressed to Protestant theologians, Patriarch Jeremias II points to Genesis 2:24 and declares that the sacrament of marriage is only confirmed in the New Testament (likewise, *Ecloga* 2:12 and the Encyclical of the Eastern Patriarchs). Indeed, Christ instituted nothing at Cana, but His presence revalues and elevates marriage to its ontological function.

Joy

The calling to mind (*anamnesis*) of Paradise is more than a simple recollection. Its redeemed grace explains a very special joy inherent to marriage: "Let us rejoice and be glad," "blessed are those who are invited to the marriage feast of the Lamb" (Rv 19:9). The Book of Deuteronomy (24:5) declares that a man who is newly married shall be freed of all obligations, including military service, in order "to bring joy to the wife he has taken." "The wife brings fullness and unending consolation to the husband," John Chrysostom says.[45] The rite constantly returns to this and sounds this clear note: "that they may rejoice," "that joy may come to them," "rejoice, O Isaiah," "and you, O bride, be exalted . . . and rejoice in your husband." One can even sense intuitively that without the nuptial love of the first couple, Paradise would lose some of its plenitude and would even be Paradise no longer! The *memoriale* of the sacrament "is mindful" of Paradise and of the Kingdom, and allows one to live some of the Edenic life on earth. This is the "grace of paradise" of which Clement speaks, which invites love to transcend the beauties of the earth for the beauty of heaven. As Paul Claudel aptly states, "The one who bears his soul within, not like a full cow ruminating on its hooves, but like a young mare, her mouth pungent with the salt she has taken from the hand of her master—how could he hold and confine this great awesome

---

[43]*In Evangelium Johannis* 9. 2.
[44]*In Danielem*, PG 56:246.
[45]*In Cap. II Geneseos Homilia* **XV**, PG 53:121, 123.

thing that rears and neighs inside the narrow stall of the personal will . . . while through the cracks in the door the wind of dawn brings the fragrance of the meadowlands" of heaven.[46]

At Cana, in the house of the first Christian couple, the Word and the Spirit preside at the feast, and for this reason one drinks the new wine, the miraculous wine that brings with it a joy not of this world. This is the "sober intoxication" of which Gregory of Nyssa speaks, and of which the Apostles were "accused" on the day of Pentecost. The nuptial Pentecost makes "all things new." The alliance of God with His people is nuptial. Jerusalem is crowned with names: the beloved of Jahweh, the Bride of the Lamb. The Service of Marriage explicitly mentions Isaiah because he sings of God's rejoicing: "No longer are you to be named Forsaken . . . for Jahweh takes delight in you . . . and as the bridegroom rejoices in the bride, so will your God rejoice in you." The joy of the sacrament is raised to the level of divine Joy.

The Minister of the Sacrament

In his *Letter to Polycarp* (5.5), Ignatius of Antioch says, "It is fitting for men and women who are marrying to form their union with the approval of the bishop."[47] The operating benediction of the priest is attested by canon seven of Neocaesarea. The bishop presides over the Eucharist and is present at the wedding feast. It is, however, at the end of the fourth century that the Church takes part directly in the marriage of the faithful. To the promise of the betrothed are added the exchange of rings, the kiss, the joining of hands by the priest, and the "common cup," *to koinon poterion*. In the second half of the third century the wedding crown appears in general use among Christians. St John Chrysostom will explain its Christian symbolism.[48] It is around this "Service of

---

[46]*La ville*, in *Théâtre* (Paris, Gallimard, 1956), p. 479-80.

[47]V. 2; *Testamentum Domini Nostri Jesu Christi* II. 1; [English translation by J. Cooper and J. A. Maclean, *The Testament of Our Lord* (London, 1902)]; *Can. Apost.* 18.

[48]*Homily IX on I Timothy.*

Crowning" that the Byzantine *Euchologion* (Service Book) structures the marriage liturgy, the *akolouthia tou stephano-matos,* and makes it the constituent element of the sacrament. In Cappadocia, in Antioch, in Constantinople, the bishops place the nuptial crown on the head of the spouses (as attested by St Gregory of Nazianzus and St John Chrysostom). In Armenia, this rite is recognized as early as the pontificate of Narses I, in the fourth century.[49] It is also recognized in Egypt.[50]

The blessing received a juridical value, and at about 895 the religious element prevailed over civil legislation, which from then on required the act of the Church in order for a marriage to be valid: "Matrimony draws its strength from the blessing [given] by the priest, so that if anyone is married without it, this marriage is null."[51] In 1092 the chrysobull of Alexius I Comnenus extended this prescription to the serfs. The Synodal Decree of Michael Anchialos in 1177 clearly states that it is not the will of the contracting parties but the sacrament that makes the marriage. In the *Treatise on the Seven Sacraments* by the monk Job the Jasite (at the end of the thirteenth century), the minister of the sacrament is the *hiereus,* the priest or the bishop. In the seventeenth century, Nicholas Bulgaris specifies in his *Catecheses* (Verona, 1681) that the matter of the sacrament is in the union of the spouses and that its form is in the blessing. In the same manner, Meletius Syrigos (Bucharest, 1690) and Metropolitan Plato of Moscow (eighteenth century) teach the unanimous doctrine: The priest is the minister of the sacrament that is instituted by God; mutual consent indicates that the betrothed are not bound by any other engagement, but that the grace results only from the rite performed. In no way, nor in any sense, can the spouses be the ministers of the sacrament. Since the thirteenth century (the Council of Lyons), and later in Peter Moghila and Patriarch Dositheus, marriage is one sacrament among the seven, and its minister is the priest.

[49]Faustus of Byzantium, I.
[50]Timothy of Alexandria, *Responsa canonica;* these canons are recognized by the Quinisext Council.
[51]*Novella* 89.

The uncommon richness of the numerous rites of the Byzantine and non-Byzantine marriage service in the Orthodox Church and the attention given to "worthily sing" its mystery clearly indicate the privileged place that the East bestows upon nuptial love.

The Sacrament of Marriage in the Byzantine Rite[52]

The following text of the Byzantine Marriage Service is as it appeared in John Meyendorff, *Marriage: an Orthodox Perspective* (New York: St Vladimir's Seminary Press, 1975), Appendix V, p. 126ff.

THE MARRIAGE SERVICE

The Service of Betrothal

The betrothal is celebrated in the narthex, or in the back part of the church.

DEACON: Bless, Master.

PRIEST: Blessed is our God, always, now and ever and unto ages of ages.

[52]Selected Bibliography a) *of Western origin:* J. H. Dalmais, "La liturgie du mariage dans les rites orientaux," in *La Maison-Dieu* (n. 50, 1957); J. Dauvillier and C. de Clercq, *Le mariage en droit canonique oriental* (Paris, 1936); M. Jugie, *Theologia dogmatica christianorum orientalium ab ecclesia Catholica dissidentium,* 5 vols., (Paris, 1926-1935); A. Raes, *Le mariage dans les Eglises d'Orient* (Chevetogne, 1958); H. Rondet, *Introduction à l'etude de la théologie du mariage* (Paris, 1960); the articles in the *Dictionnaire de théologie catholique;* [K. Ritzer, *Le marriage dans les Eglises chrétiennes du Ier au XIe siècle* (Paris, 1970); b) *of Eastern origin:* Anthony Coniaris, *These are the Sacraments* (1981), p. 127ff.; Casimir Kucharek, *The Sacramental Mysteries. A Byzantine Approach* (1976), p. 302ff., and *The Rite of Holy Matrimony According to the Byzantine Slav Rite;* John Meyendorff, *Marriage: an Orthodox Perspective* (New York, 1975); "A Symposium on the Meaning of Marriage," in *St Vladimir's Seminary Quarterly* (vol. 8, n. 1, 1964)—ed.]

CHOIR: Amen.

DEACON: In peace let us pray to the Lord.

CHOIR: Lord, have mercy. (*Repeated after each petition.*)

DEACON: For the peace from above and for the salvation of our souls, let us pray to the Lord.

For the peace of the whole world, for the welfare of the holy churches of God, and for the union of all, let us pray to the Lord.

For this holy house and for those who enter with faith, reverence, and the fear of God, let us pray to the Lord.

For our Metropolitan ————, for our Bishop ————, for the honorable priesthood, the diaconate in Christ, for all the clergy and the people, let us pray to the Lord.

For the servant of God ————, and for the handmaiden of God ————, who now plight each other their troth, and for their salvation, let us pray to the Lord.

That they may be granted children for the continuation of the race, and all their petitions which are unto salvation, let us pray to the Lord.

That He will send down upon them perfect and peaceful love, and assistance, let us pray to the Lord.

That He will preserve them in oneness of mind, and in steadfast faith, let us pray to the Lord.

That He will preserve them in a blameless way of life, let us pray to the Lord.

That the Lord our God will grant to them an honorable marriage and a bed undefiled, let us pray to the Lord.

For our deliverance from all affliction, wrath, danger, and necessity, let us pray to the Lord.

Help us, save us, have mercy on us, and keep us, O God, by Thy grace.

DEACON: Commemorating our most holy, most pure, most blessed and glorious Lady Theotokos and ever-virgin Mary, with all the saints, let us commend ourselves and each other, and all our life unto Christ our God.

CHOIR: To Thee, O Lord.

DEACON: For unto Thee are due all glory, honor, and worship: to the Father, and to the Son, and to the Holy Spirit now, and ever and unto ages of ages.

CHOIR: Amen.

PRIEST: O eternal God, who hast brought into unity those who were sundered, and hast ordained for them an indissoluble bond of love, who didst bless Isaac and Rebecca, and didst make them heirs of Thy promise: Bless also these Thy servants, ————— and ————, guiding them unto every good work. For Thou art a good God and lovest mankind, and unto Thee we ascribe glory: to the Father, and to the Son, and to the Holy Spirit, now and ever and unto ages of ages.

CHOIR: Amen.

PRIEST: Peace be unto all.

CHOIR: And to your spirit.

DEACON: Bow your heads unto the Lord.

CHOIR: To Thee, O Lord.

PRIEST: O Lord our God, who hast espoused the Church as a pure virgin from among the gentiles: Bless this betrothal, and unite and maintain these Thy servants in peace and oneness of mind. For unto Thee are due all glory, honor, and worship: to the Father, and to the Son, and to the Holy Spirit, now and ever and unto ages of ages.

CHOIR: Amen.

Then taking the rings, the priest blesses the bridal pair, making the sign of the cross with the ring of the bride over the bridegroom, and with that of the bridegroom over the bride, saying to the man: The servant of God, ————, is betrothed to the handmaiden of God, ————, in the name of the Father, and of the Son, and of the Holy Spirit. Amen.

And to the woman: The handmaiden of God, ————, is betrothed to the servant of God, ————, in the name of the Father, and of the Son, and of the Holy Spirit. Amen.

And when he has said this to each of them three times, he places the rings on their right hands. Then the bridal pair exchanges the rings, and the priest says the following prayer.

DEACON: Let us pray to the Lord.

CHOIR: Lord, have mercy.

PRIEST: O Lord our God, who didst accompany the servant of the patriarch Abraham into Mesopotamia, when he was sent to espouse a wife for his lord Isaac, and who, by means of the drawing of water, didst reveal to him that he should betroth Rebecca. Do Thou, the same Lord, bless also the betrothal of these Thy servants, ———— and ————, and confirm the promise that they have made. Establish them in the holy union which is from Thee. For in the beginning Thou didst make them male and female, and by Thee the woman is joined unto the man as a helper and for the procreation of the human race. Therefore, O Lord our God, who hast sent forth Thy truth upon Thine inheritance, and Thy covenant unto Thy servants our fathers, Thine

elect from generation to generation: Look upon
Thy servant, —————, and Thy handmaiden,
—————, and establish and make firm their
betrothal, in faith and in oneness of mind, in
truth and in love. For Thou, O Lord, hast declared
that a pledge should be given and confirmed in all
things. By a ring power was given to Joseph in
Egypt; by a ring Daniel was glorified in the land
of Babylon; by a ring the uprightness of Tamar
was revealed; by a ring our heavenly Father showed
His bounty upon His Son, for He said: Bring the
fatted calf and kill it, and let us eat and make
merry. By Thine own right hand, O Lord, Thou
didst arm Moses in the Red Sea; by Thy true word
the heavens were established, and the foundations
of the earth were made firm, and the right hands of
Thy servants also shall be blessed by Thy mighty
word and by Thine upraised arm. Therefore, O
Master, bless now this putting-on of rings with
Thy heavenly blessing, and let Thine angel go before them all the days of their life. For Thou art
He that blesses and sanctifies all things, and unto
Thee are due all glory, honor, and worship to the
Father, and to the Son, and to the Holy Spirit, now
and ever and unto ages of ages.

CHOIR: Amen.

The Service of Crowning

*The bridal couple, preceded by the Priest, moves in procession
to the center of the church.*

PRIEST AND CHOIR, *Refrain:* Glory to Thee, our God, glory
to Thee!

Blessed is every one who fears the Lord, who walks
in his ways!

You shall eat the fruit of the labor of your hands,
you shall be happy, and it shall be well with you.

Your wife will be like a fruitful vine within your
house;

your children will be like olive shoots around your
table.
Lo, thus shall the man be blessed who fears the
Lord.

The Lord bless you from Zion!

May you see the prosperity of Jerusalem all the
days of your life!

May you see your children's children!

Peace be upon Israel! (Ps 128)

[An exhortation may follow. Then according to Slavonic editions of the marriage service, the priest shall inquire of the bridegroom: Do you, —————, have a good, free, and unconstrained will and a firm intention to take as your wife this woman, —————, whom you see here before you?

BRIDEGROOM: I have, reverend father.

PRIEST: Have you promised yourself to any other bride?

BRIDEGROOM: I have not promised myself, reverend father.

And the priest, looking at the bride, shall inquire of her: Do you, —————, have a good, free, and unconstrained will and a firm intention to take as your husband this man, —————, whom you see here before you?

BRIDE: I have, reverend father.

PRIEST: Have you promised yourself to any other man?

BRIDE: I have not promised myself, reverend father.]

DEACON: Bless, master.

PRIEST: Blessed is the Kingdom of the Father, and of the
           Son, and of the Holp Spirit, now and ever and unto
           ages of ages.

CHOIR: Amen.

DEACON: In peace let us pray to the Lord.

CHOIR: Lord, have mercy. (*Repeated after each petition.*)

DEACON: For the peace from above and for the salvation
           of our souls, let us pray to the Lord.

           For the peace of the whole world, for the welfare
           of the holy churches of God, and for the union
           of all, let us pray to the Lord.

           For this holy house and for those who enter with
           faith, reverence, and the fear of God, let us pray
           to the Lord.

           For our Metropolitan ————, for our Bishop
           ————, for the honorable priesthood, the di-
           aconate in Christ, for all the clergy and the people,
           let us pray to the Lord.

           For the servants of God, ———— and ————,
           who are now being united to each other in the
           community of marriage, and for their salvation,
           let us pray to the Lord.

           That He will bless this marriage, as He blessed
           the marriage in Cana of Galilee, let us pray to the
           Lord.

           That He will grant to them chastity, and the fruit
           of the womb as is expedient for them, let us pray
           to the Lord.

           That He will make them glad with the sight of
           sons and daughters, let us pray to the Lord.

           That He will grant to them enjoyment of the
           blessing of children, and a blameless life, let us
           pray to the Lord.

That He will grant to them and to us, all our petitions which are unto salvation, let us pray to the Lord.

That He will deliver them and us from all affliction, wrath, danger, and necessity, let us pray to the Lord.

Help us, save us, have mercy on us, and keep us O God, by Thy grace.

DEACON: Commemorating our most holy, most pure, most blessed and glorious Lady Theotokos and ever-virgin Mary, with all the saints, let us command ourselves and each other, and all our life unto Christ our God.

CHOIR: To Thee, O Lord.

PRIEST: For unto Thee are due all glory, honor, and worship: to the Father, and to the Son, and to the Holy Spirit, now and ever and unto ages of ages.

CHOIR: Amen.

DEACON: Let us pray to the Lord.

CHOIR: Lord, have mercy.

Then the priest recites aloud the following prayer: O God most pure, fashioner of every creature, who didst transform the rib of our forefather Adam into a wife, because of Thy love toward mankind, and didst bless them and say to them: Be fruitful and multiply, and fill the earth and subdue it; who didst make of the two one flesh: Therefore a man leaves his father and his mother and cleaves to his wife, and the two shall become one flesh, and what God has joined together, let no man put asunder. Thou didst bless Thy servant Abraham, and opening the womb of Sarah didst make him to be the father of many nations. Thou didst give Isaac to Rebecca, and didst bless her in childbear-

ing. Thou didst join Jacob unto Rachel, and from
them didst bring forth the twelve patriarchs. Thou
didst unite Joseph and Aseneth, giving to them
Ephraim and Manasseh as the fruit of their procreation. Thou didst accept Zechariah and Elizabeth,
and didst make their offspring to be the Forerunner.
From the root of Jesse according to the flesh, Thou
didst put forth the ever-virgin one, and wast incarnate of her, and wast born of her for the redemption of the human race. Through Thine unutterable gift and manifold goodness, Thou didst
come to Cana of Galilee, and didst bless the marriage there, to make manifest that it is Thy will
that there should be lawful marriage and procreation. Do Thou, the same all-holy Master, accept
the prayers of us Thy servants. As Thou wast
present there, be Thou also present here, with
Thine invisible protection. Bless this marriage, and
grant to these Thy servants, ———— and
————, a peaceful life, length of days, chastity,
mutual love in the bond of peace, long-lived offspring, gratitude from their children, a crown of
glory that does not fade away. Graciously grant
that they may see their children's children. Preserve their bed unassailed, and give them of the
dew of heaven from on high, and of the fatness
of the earth. Fill their houses with wheat, wine
and oil and with every good thing, so that they
may give in turn to those in need; and grant also
to those here present with them all those petitions
that are for their salvation. For Thou art the God
of mercies, and of bounties, and of love toward
mankind, and unto Thee we ascribe glory: to the
Father, and to the Son, and to the Holy Spirit, now
and ever and unto ages of ages.

CHOIR: Amen.

DEACON: Let us pray to the Lord.

CHOIR: Lord, have mercy.

Then the priest recites aloud the following prayer: Blessed art Thou, O Lord our God, priest of mystical and undefiled marriage, and ordainer of the law of the marriage of the body; preserver of immortality, and provider of the good things of life; the same master who in the beginning didst make man and establish him as a king over creation, and didst say: "It is not good that man should be alone upon the earth. Let us make a helper fit for him." Taking one of his ribs, Thou didst fashion woman; and when Adam saw her he said: "This is at last bone of my bones and flesh of my flesh; she shall be called Woman, because she was taken out of Man." For this reason a man shall leave his father and mother and be joined to his wife, and the two shall become one flesh; what therefore God has joined together, let no man put asunder: Do Thou now also, O Master, our Lord and our God, send down Thy heavenly grace upon these Thy Servants, —————— and ——————; grant that this Thy handmaiden may be subject to her husband in all things, and that this Thy servant may be the head of his wife, so that they may live according to Thy will. Bless them, O Lord our God, as Thou didst bless Abraham and Sarah. Bless them, O Lord our God, as Thou didst bless Isaac and Rebecca. Bless them, O Lord our God, as Thou didst bless Jacob and all the patriarchs. Bless them, O Lord our God, as Thou didst bless Joseph and Aseneth. Bless them, O Lord our God, as Thou didst bless Moses and Zipporah. Bless them, O Lord our God, as Thou didst bless Joachim and Anna. Bless them, O Lord our God, as Thou didst bless Zechariah and Elizabeth. Preserve them, O Lord our God, as Thou didst preserve Noah in the ark. Preserve them, O Lord our God, as Thou didst preserve Jonah in the belly of the whale. Preserve them, O Lord our

God, as Thou didst preserve the three holy children
from the fire, sending down upon them dew from
heaven; and let that gladness come upon them that
the blessed Helen had when she found the precious
cross. Remember them, O Lord our God, as Thou
didst remember Enoch, Shem, Elijah. Remember
them, O Lord our God, as Thou didst remember
Thy forty holy martyrs, sending down upon them
crowns from heaven. Remember them, O Lord our
God, and the parents who have nurtured them, for
the prayers of parents make firm the foundations
of houses. Remember, O Lord our God, Thy servants the groomsman and the bridesmaid of the
bridal pair, who have come together in this joy.
Remember, O Lord our God, Thy servant,
—————, and Thy handmaiden, —————, and
bless them. Grant them of the fruit of their
bodies, fair children, concord of soul and body.
Exalt them like the cedars of Lebanon, like a
luxuriant vine. Give them offspring in number like
unto full ears of grain, so that having enough of
all things, they may abound in every work that is
good and acceptable unto Thee. Let them see their
children's children, like olive shoots around their
table, so that finding favor in Thy sight, they may
shine like the stars of heaven, in Thee our God.
For unto Thee are due all glory, honor, and worship: to the Father, and to the Son, and to the Holy
Spirit, now and ever and unto ages of ages.

CHOIR: Amen.

DEACON: Let us pray to the Lord.

CHOIR: Lord, have mercy.

And again the priest prays aloud: O holy God, who didst
form man from the dust, and didst fashion woman
from his rib, and didst join her unto him as a
helper, for it seemed good to Thy majesty that
man should not be alone upon the earth: Do Thou,

the same Lord, stretch out now also Thy hand from Thy holy dwelling place, and unite this Thy servant, —————, and this Thy handmaiden, —————; for by Thee is the husband joined unto the wife. Unite them in one mind; wed them into one flesh, granting to them the fruit of the body and the procreation of fair children. For Thine is the majesty, and Thine is the Kingdom and the power and the glory: of the Father, and of the Son, and of the Holy Spirit, now and ever and unto ages of ages.

CHOIR: Amen.

The priest takes the crowns, which recall those with which the "martyrs," or witnesses of Christ, are crowned in heaven, and crowns first the bridegroom, saying: The servant of God, —————, is crowned unto the handmaiden of God, —————, in the name of the Father, and of the Son, and of the Holy Spirit.

So also he crowns the bride, saying: The handmaiden of God, —————, is crowned unto the servant of God, —————, in the name of the Father, and of the Son, and of the Holy Spirit.

Then he blesses them three times, saying each time: O Lord our God, crown them with glory and honor.

DEACON: Let us attend.

PRIEST: Peace be unto all.

READER: And to your spirit.

DEACON: Wisdom!

READER: The prokeimenon in the eighth tone (Ps 21): Thou hast set upon their heads crowns of precious stones; they asked life of Thee, and Thou gavest it them.

Yea, Thou wilt make them most blessed for ever;

Thou wilt make them glad with the joy of Thy presence.

DEACON: Wisdom!

READER: The reading is from the Epistle of the holy Apostle Paul to the Ephesians.

DEACON: Let us attend.

READER: (Eph 5:20-33) Brethren: Give thanks always and for everything in the name of our Lord Jesus Christ to God the Father. Be subject to one another out of reverence for Christ. Wives, be subject to your husbands, as to the Lord. For the husband is the head of the wife as Christ is the head of the church, His body, and is Himself its Savior. As the church is subject to Christ, so let wives also be subject in everything to their husbands. Husbands, love your wives, as Christ loved the church and gave Himself up for her, that He might sanctify her, having cleansed her by the washing of water with the word, that the church might be presented before Him in splendor, without spot or wrinkle or any such thing, that she might be holy and without blemish. Even so husbands should love their wives as their own bodies. He who loves his wife loves himself. For no man ever hates his own flesh, but nourishes and cherishes it, as Christ does the church, because we are members of His body. "For this reason a man shall leave his father and mother and be joined to his wife, and the two shall become one." This is a great mystery, and I take it to mean Christ and the church; however, let each one of you love his wife as himself and let the wife see that she respects her husband.

PRIEST: Peace be unto you, reader.

READER: And to your spirit, Alleluia! Alleluia! Alleluia!

VERSE: (Ps 12:7; tone 5): Thou, O Lord, shalt protect us and preserve us from this generation forever.

PRIEST: Peace be unto all.

CHOIR: And to your spirit.

PRIEST: The reading from the Holy Gospel according to Saint John.

CHOIR: Glory to Thee, O Lord, glory to Thee.

DEACON: Let us attend.

PRIEST: (Jn 2:1-11) In those days there was a marriage at Cana in Galilee, and the mother of Jesus was there; Jesus also was invited to the marriage, with His disciples. When the wine failed, the mother of Jesus said to Him, "They have no wine." And Jesus said to her, "O woman, what have you to do with me? My hour has not yet come." His mother said to the servants, "Do whatever He tells you." Now six stone jars were standing there, for the Jewish rites of purification, each holding twenty or thirty gallons. Jesus said to them, "Fill the jars with water." And they filled them up to the brim. He said to them, "Now draw some out, and take it to the steward of the feast." So they took it. When the steward of the feast tasted the water now become wine, and did not know where it came from (though the servants who had drawn the water knew), the steward of the feast called the bridegroom and said to him, "Every man serves the good wine first, and when men have drunk freely, then the poor wine; but you have kept the good wine until now." This, the first of His signs, Jesus did at Cana in Galilee, and manifested His glory, and His disciples believed in Him.

CHOIR: Glory to Thee, O Lord, glory to Thee.

DEACON: Let us all say with all our soul and with all our mind, let us say.

CHOIR: Lord, have mercy.

DEACON: O Lord almighty, the God of our Fathers, we pray Thee, hearken and have mercy.

CHOIR: Lord, have mercy.

DEACON: Have mercy on us, O God, according to Thy great goodness, we pray Thee, hearken and have mercy.

CHOIR: Lord, have mercy. (3)

DEACON: Again we pray for mercy, life, peace, health, salvation, and visitation for the servants of God. _____ and _____ (*and he mentions also whomever else he wishes*), and for the pardon and remission of their sins.

CHOIR: Lord, have mercy. (3)

PRIEST: For Thou art a merciful God, and lovest mankind and unto Thee we ascribe glory: to the Father and to the Son, and to the Holy Spirit, now and ever and unto ages of ages.

CHOIR: Amen.

DEACON: Let us pray to the Lord.

CHOIR: Lord, have mercy.

PRIEST: O Lord our God, who in Thy saving dispensation didst vouchsafe by Thy presence in Cana of Galilee to declare marriage honorable: Do Thou, the same Lord, now also maintain in peace and concord Thy servants, _____ and _____, whom Thou hast been pleased to join together. Cause their marriage to be honorable. Preserve their bed blameless. Mercifully grant that they may live together in purity; and enable them to reach a ripe old age, walking in Thy commandments with a pure heart. For Thou art our God, the God of mercy and salvation, and unto Thee we ascribe glory: to the Father, and to the Son, and to the Holy Spirit, now and ever unto ages of ages.

CHOIR: Amen.

DEACON: Help us, save us, have mercy on us, and keep us, O God, by Thy grace.

CHOIR: Lord, have mercy.

DEACON: That the whole day may be perfect, holy, peaceful, and sinless, let us ask of the Lord.

CHOIR: Grant it, O Lord. (*Repeated after each petition.*)

DEACON: An angel of peace, a faithful guide, a guardian of our souls and bodies, let us ask of the Lord.

Pardon and remission of our sins and transgressions, let us ask of the Lord.

All things that are good and profitable for our souls, and peace for the world, let us ask of the Lord.

That we may complete the remaining time of our life in peace and repentance, let us ask of the Lord.

A Christian ending to our life: painless, blameless, and peaceful; and a good defense before the dread judgment seat of Christ, let us ask of the Lord.

DEACON: Having asked for the unity of the Faith, and the communion of the Holy Spirit, let us commend ourselves and each other, and all our life unto Christ our God.

CHOIR: To Thee, O Lord.

PRIEST: And make us worthy, O Master, that with boldness and without condemnation we may dare to call on Thee, the heavenly God, as Father, and to say:

CHOIR: Our Father, who art in heaven, hallowed be Thy name. Thy Kingdom come, Thy will be done, on earth as it is in heaven. Give us this day our daily bread; and forgive us our trespasses, as we forgive those who trespass against us; and lead us not into temptation, but deliver us from evil.

PRIEST: For Thine is the Kingdom, and the power, and the glory: of the Father, and of the Son, and of the Holy Spirit, now and ever and unto ages of ages.

CHOIR: Amen.

PRIEST: Peace be unto all.

CHOIR: And to your spirit.

DEACON: Bow your heads unto the Lord.

CHOIR: To Thee, O Lord.

Then the common cup is brought and the priest blesses it.

DEACON: Let us pray to the Lord.

CHOIR: Lord, have mercy.

PRIEST: O God, who hast created all things by Thy might, and hast made firm the world, and adornest the crown of all that Thou hast made: Bless now, with Thy spiritual blessing, this common cup, which Thou dost give to those who are now united for the community of marriage. For blessed is Thy name, and glorified is Thy Kingdom, of the Father, and of the Son, and of the Holy Spirit, now and ever and unto ages of ages.

CHOIR: Amen.

Then, taking the cup, the priest gives it to them three times; first to the bridegroom and then to the bride. Then immediately the priest takes them, the groomsmen behind them holding their crowns, and leads them in a circle three times around the lectern. And the priest or the choir sings:

Rejoice, O Isaiah! A virgin is with child; and shall bear a Son, Emmanuel. He is both God and man; and Orient is His name. Magnifying Him, we call the virgin blessed.

O holy martyrs, who fought the good fight and have received your crowns: Entreat ye the Lord, that He will have mercy on our souls.

Glory to Thee, O Christ God, the apostles' boast, the martyrs' joy whose preaching was the consubstantial Trinity.

Then, taking the crown of the bridegroom, the priest says: Be exalted like Abraham, O Bridegroom, and be blessed like Isaac, and multiply like Jacob, walking in peace, and keeping God's commandments in righteousness.

Then, taking the crown of the bride, he says: And you, O bride: Be exalted like Sarah, and exult like Rebecca, and multiply like Rachel, and rejoice in your husband, fulfilling the conditions of the law, for this is well-pleasing to God.

DEACON: Let us pray to the Lord.

CHOIR: Lord, have mercy.

PRIEST: O God, our God, who didst come to Cana of Galilee, and didst bless there the marriage feast: Bless also these Thy servants, who through Thy good providence now are united in wedlock. Bless their goings out and their comings in. Fill their life with good things. Receive their crowns into Thy Kingdom, preserving them spotless, blameless, and without reproach, unto ages of ages.

CHOIR: Amen.

PRIEST: Peace be unto all.

CHOIR: And to your spirit.

DEACON: Bow your heads unto the Lord.

CHOIR: To Thee, O Lord.

PRIEST: May the Father, and the Son, and the Holy Spirit, the all-holy, consubstantial, and life-giving Trinity, one Godhead and one Kingdom, bless you; and grant you length of days, fair children, progress in life and faith; and fill you with all earthly good things, and make you worthy to enjoy the good things of the promise; through the prayers of the holy Theotokos and of all the saints. Amen.

DEACON: Most holy Theotokos, save us!

CHOIR: More honorable than the Cherubim, and more glorious beyond compare than the Seraphim; without defilement you gave birth to God the Word: true Theotokos, we magnify you.

PRIEST: Glory to Thee, O Christ our God and our hope, glory to Thee.

CHOIR: Glory to the Father, and to the Son, and to the Holy Spirit, now and ever and unto ages of ages. Amen. Lord have mercy. (3) Father, bless.

PRIEST: May He who by His presence in Cana of Galilee declared marriage to be honorable, Christ our true God, through the prayers of His most pure mother; of the holy, glorious, and all-laudable apostles; of the holy, God-crowned kings Constantine and Helen, equal to the apostles, of the holy great martyr Procopius; and of all the saints; have mercy on us and save us, for He is good and loves mankind.

CHOIR: Amen.

Brief Commentary on the Sacrament of Marriage

The betrothal occurs with the exchange of rings, hence the name of "the service of the rings," *akolouthia tou arrabonos.* The "service of crowning," *akolouthia tou stephanomatos,* follows as a rule immediately afterward and consists of the imposition of the crowns. Both services are therefore celebrated during the course of the same ceremony.

After the Divine Liturgy, during which they receive Holy Communion, the betrothed stand before the royal Door, the man facing the icon of Christ and the woman facing the icon of the Theotokos (the symbol of the Church). They turn their thoughts to this archetypal image of marriage, which according to St Paul is the union of Christ with the Church.

The two rings are placed in the heart of the sanctuary, on the altar table; thus they are touching the mystery of the Kingdom and, as symbols of a new destiny, they indicate the dimension into which the sacrament will lead the couple.

The priest receives from the betrothed the assurance that they present themselves in complete freedom before the eyes of God. He blesses them with the lighted nuptial candles, which they will hold throughout the service; their light is reminiscent of what was in the beginning, "Let there be light." The light goes back to the prelapsarian plan of creation and to the paradisiacal word of institution of the nuptial union. Their flames are also a reminder of the Pentecostal fire; the betrothed are awaiting the descent of grace, their nuptial Pentecost.

The priest censes the betrothed, in the form of a cross. This symbolic gesture refers to the Tobias story: the smoke chased away the demons and made the place pure and holy. At the threshold of a new life the sign of the cross is made, with its power to protect. The cross purified the air and freed the cosmos from domination by demons, as St Athanasius teaches.[53]

After the litanies, the priest recites the first prayer, "O eternal God . . . ,"[54] asking that the grace of God bring together what has been sundered and make the bond of love indissoluble. In it, we hear echoes of the oldest eucharistic prayer of the *Didache*: "As this broken bread was scattered upon the mountains, but was brought together and became one, so let thy Church be gathered together from the ends of the earth."[55] In its very inspiration, the love of the betrothed

[53]*Vita Sancti Athanasii*, PG 25:140AC.

[54]These two prayers are found in the Barberini Codex 336, of the eighth century, although they are much older.

[55]*Didache* 9.2, trans. Kirsopp Lake, in *The Apostolic Fathers* (The Loeb Classical Library, 1959), p. 323.

is linked to and oriented toward eucharistic communion.

The second prayer places us before the divine archetype of matrimony, the espousals of Christ to the Church. Its breadth echoes the inspired words of St John Chrysostom, that marriage is not the image of something earthly! The Coptic ritual mentions here the story of Eleazar, Abraham's steward. God accompanies him on his journey and reveals to him the means of recognizing the chosen one. In this way God directs the steps of those who will meet with another; His design for the lovers is the pledge of His blessings.

The third prayer is no less filled with meaning. It interprets the significance of the puttting on of rings. The meaning of their putting on and of their exchange between the betrothed becomes considerably more profound in the Armenian and Syrian rites where, according to a very ancient usage, the exchange of baptismal crosses is a clear symbolic expression of the mutual surrender of one's destiny.[56] The Syrian rite begins at the highest point: "How many mysteries are hidden and contained in the spendor of the rings! . . . Our Lord Jesus Christ who is betrothed to the Church and who, through His blood, has established a dowry for her, and has forged for her a ring with the nails of His crucifixion . . ."

The prayer of the Byzantine rite speaks of Joseph: the royal seal inserted in the claw of the ring was the sign of his power and a pledge confirming the pharaoh's trust and fidelity toward him. Likewise, in the evocation of the story of Daniel thrown into the lions' den, the king affixed his seal, which assured the prophet's liberation and signified the same pledge of fidelity toward him. Tamar, called before the judge Judah, shows the ring which reminds the judge of his promise and obliges him to be true to it. Finally, when the prodigal son returns home, the father places the ring on his finger, a sign of the pardon that was granted and of the royal dignity that was restored.

The encounter of the betrothed is sealed as it were by the ring of the divine promise. This is a summary of the history of humanity: the child of God is saved through the

[56]See canon XIII of the Nestorian Synod of Katar in 677. Cf. Chabot, *Synodicon orientale* (Paris, 1902).

faithfulness of the Father, the Philanthropist, "the lover of mankind." The divine act is followed at once by a royal gift: "let Thine angel go before them all the days of their life." This is a striking symbolism of the unity in one being, a single destiny: the angel of the nuptial community leads it to the Kingdom.[57]

*   *   *

In the West, the ancient Roman Liturgy contained the rite of *velatio,* which stressed the Pauline image of the "veil," the symbol of femininity, of its reserve and submission. In the East, married women commonly wore veils. The Eastern rite of crowning suppresses, removes, the veil and stresses the royal freedom of the spouses and their equality in the mutual gift of self. The dignity of the woman as the companion and equal of her partner is brought out more strongly; the two incorporate the one and only image of God.

The Service of Crowning begins with the singing of Psalm 127 (128), which has been part of the wedding ceremony since the fourth century. It was sung on account of its ending, and one should understand its hidden meaning well. The same words are found in the central prayer of the sacrament of anointing (chrismation): "The Lord bless you from Zion. May you see the prosperity of Jerusalem all the days of your life." The full, priestly consecration of a life to the service of God ends with a clearly eschatological vision; the reference is indeed to the heavenly Jerusalem. Likewise, the singing of Psalm 127 (128) calls upon God, asking that His blessings be sent from Zion. This name signifies both "place of salvation" (Is 46:13) and Jerusalem, a synonym of the messianic Kingdom, which rabbinic and apocalyptic literature would call "the heavenly Jerusalem," the spouse of God. After Palm Sunday, Jerusalem points toward Christ and His glorified body, the mystical Church, the place where the history of salvation is enacted.

From the very beginning, this profound reminder raises

---

[57]In iconography, the angel of marriage wears a cerulean vestment, symbol of heavenly integrity. See F. Portal, *Les couleurs symboliques* (Paris, 1837).

the bridal pair above the horizons of the earth. It teaches the steadfast and only true nuptial attitude: at every moment, "every day of his life," man, on earth, looks to the East; through his roots his joy drinks from heaven. The espousals on earth are the beginning of the ascension of Zion in the Taboric light.

The prayers that follow the diaconal liturgy mention the names of the patriarchs and the blessings granted them, bringing together the two covenants in a single economy of salvation. The events reported illustrate and glorify the unswerving faithfulness of God. The impressive procession of patriarchs ends with Zechariah and Elizabeth on the one hand, and Joachim and Anna on the other. These are the couples that brought forth the human archetypes: the masculine, John the Baptist, and the feminine, the Virgin, the "unmarried spouse," "from whom the Savior is born without the intermediary of marriage," the royal bridegroom of the banquet of the wise virgins. Marriage is thereby placed under the signs of the miraculous Birth, and of the Servant and the Friend of the one Bridegroom.

This is why the prayers return on several occasions to a petition for *nuptial chastity* and a marriage bed unassailed. They evoke the wedding at Cana and lead to the symbolism of transfigured love, rendered charismatic. The revealing encounter of virginity and the nuptial state discloses the same source and the same fullness, where, since the wedding at Cana, the two mysteries of human life conclude.

This is reinforced by reference to Enoch, Elijah, and Shem. God carried these prophets to heaven alive; one tradition also affirms this in the case of Shem, the son of Noah. That they are mentioned is important: those who unite themselves are placed before the human prefiguration of the Ascension of the Lord; earthly horizons in no way limit the shared ascension of the married.

This marvelous balance of heaven and earth leads us back to concrete existence. On the evening of great feasts, the priest blesses wheat, wine, and oil, which are figures and present examples of the fruits of the earth, the *alma mater*. Starting from this schematic point, the benediction extends

over the entire universe and sanctifies its fecundity, of which
man is the master-steward. The prayer of the ceremony of
marriage quotes the same formula and specifies at once the
goal of the things of this earth: "so that they may give in
turn to those in need . . . for their salvation." The abundance
of the joy of the feast rectifies and sensitizes man's attention,
makes him open, and predisposes him to show compassion
to those who are lonely, who suffer and feel abandoned, far
from God. From now on, the spouses are for everyone a
"Thou"; they are for all this the beggar who is rich in God,
and the poor brother of all the people whose salvation He
ardently desires.

The first prayer of the Service of Crowning invokes,
clarifies, and makes the wedding at Cana present: "Through
Thine unutterable gift Thou didst come to Cana of Galilee,
and didst bless the marriage there, to make manifest that it
is Thy will that there should be lawful marriage . . . Accept
the prayers of us Thy servants. As Thou wast present there,
be Thou also present here."

In the Gospel, every work of Christ reaches completion
in glory; its fulfillment is manifested and glorified by the
Holy Spirit. Standing in the presence of Christ, the betrothed
receive the glory that achieves the establishment of their
unique being, and the priest raises them to this glory through
the invocation (*epiklesis*) of the sacrament: "O Lord our
God, crown them with glory and honor." This is the effective
moment of the sacrament, the time of the nuptial Pentecost,
the descent of the Holy Spirit making a new creation.

The Coptic ritual strongly emphasizes this meaning
through the anointing of the betrothed, a reminder of the
anointing with chrism and a sign of the Pentecostal gifts. The
prayer over the oil reads: "Thou who hast anointed priests,
kings, and prophets [the threefold dignity of the royal Priest-
hood] with the product of the olive tree, we ask Thee to
bring Thy blessing upon the oil here present. Let it be an oil
of sanctification, an oil of chastity, a light and a beauty without blemish." The choir sings, "it is the oil of the holy
spirits . . ." The anointing infuses the grace of *married holiness*. What was separated is no longer; the angel of the

nuptial being is present as a heavenly witness of the creative word reconstituted and heard anew: "He made *him* in the likeness of God. He created *them* . . . and gave *them* the name of Man." This wonderful parallelism to liturgical gladness makes us feel how strongly the words of the priestly prayer of Christ ("I have given them glory . . . that they may be one" [Jn 17:22]) are present at the heart of the same glory manifested at Cana. And it is present at every Christian wedding. It is the very formula of nuptial love and the sacrament of marriage.

The central prayer at the Service of Crowning is very revealing; it is placed at the beginning and at the end of man's destiny, and unifies them. Indeed, while describing the magnificence of innocent man at the beginning of life, the Epistle to the Hebrews (2:7) says, "You *have crowned him with glory and honor.*" The Book of Revelation is placed at the other extreme, at the end of history, and closes with the vision of the new city, "into which the nations shall bring their glory and honor." Men do not reach the shores of the Kingdom empty-handed; they carry the gifts of the Spirit, glory and honor. But the same formula that expresses the initial promise and its fulfillment (Paradise and the Kingdom) is now placed as the words that constitute the sacrament: the spouses are crowned with glory and honor. In this manner, marriage appears as the point where the alpha and the omega of human destiny meet.

The Service of Crowning is introduced by reminding us of the forty martyrs of Sebaste to whom God sent crowns from heaven. The mention of St Procopius is also revealing. His *Vita* relates how he had exhorted the spouses to reach marriage in heaven through martyrdom. This brief summary orients the procession-wedding dance, and with the troparion of the martyrs ("O holy martyrs who fought the good fight and have received your crowns, entreat ye the Lord, that He will have mercy on our souls") leads it to the same goal, indicating the glorious end of life's pilgrimage. Through their love for each other, the couple causes this magnificent prayer of the martyrs to well up: "It is you, my spouse, whom I desire. In searching for you I struggle and I am crucified with you. I am buried with you in baptism, and I suffer with you only to live with you." The setting of ancient wedding rings showed two profiles joined by a cross. Perfect love is love crucified. This is why the crowns refer to the Lord's crown of thorns, the only one that can give meaning to all others. Throughout their entire life, the spouses will hear echoes, strong or dim, of the Troparion of the Holy Martyrs.

St John Chrysostom sees in the crown the symbol of nuptial asceticism, in order to obtain chastity, integrity of being. It is noteworthy that the Service contains no fear of the woman, no trace of suspicion or of contempt. The prayer for nuptial chastity is the opposite of every concept advancing "a remedy for concupiscence"; it asks for something entirely different, the miracle of the transfiguration of Eros. Carnal sin is not at all *sin of the flesh,* but sin of the spirit *against the flesh,* the profanation of the sacred and of the sanctity of the Incarnation. The various ways offered by the sacrament to conquer instinctive sexuality point to new possibilities from which love emerges eternally young, new, and virginal, purified of the stigma of an adulterous past.

The sexual freedom of the modern world, paradoxically and through violent contrast, points to a secret desire for purity and covering. The grandeur of the nuptial community calls for the victory not of a tyrant who measures out and weighs love and ends by suppressing it, but for a master and lord who has the power to transform it. Against the drab background of modern eroticism, surfeited and sunk in gargantuan boredom, love once again stands out as the one great, fascinating adventure through which man touches heaven not simply in poetry, but ontologically, through the charism of nuptial holiness.

Certain ancient manuscripts, as well as a sketch of an icon of St Michael, present Satan with two faces, one of which is placed below the navel, symbolic of the splitting and dissociation of the personality through demonic concupiscence. This is the ultimate perversion of the principle of virginity. Concupiscence requires the deep sacramental penetration of human nature. This is why marriage is a *sacrament,* to recapture the chastity that has been lost. Clement of Alexandria speaks of the "Paradisiacal grace" that gives the initial integrity (*sophrosyne*) back to the human spirit. According to ancient tradition, one waited for the seventh day to remove the symbolic crowns. These seven days of continence initiated self-control in man and served as a monastic novitiate: they were spent in prayer in order to prepare for the mystery of love.[58] "It is not the path that is difficult: it is the difficult that is the path." This utterance of Kierkegaard can be applied to the awesome dignity of marriage.

Love is mysterious. It comes suddenly but it can also depart suddenly; its ebb, and eventual disappearance, are even more incomprehensible than its birth. Natural love, love secularized, is a defenseless victim of human inconstancy. No word that is merely human ever keeps its promises. "Love" and "always" only make sense in the poetry of the "first morning." We now understand the tireless insistence on the *sacrament* of marriage which asks for the miracle, the charism, and without ceasing prays for "perfect love," "the indissoluble bond," "mutual love and tender friendship." The Chaldean liturgy prays, "O Lord. inflame these lovers with the fire of love; in the morning of all your days, may you awake unto joy! . . . When you extend your right hand, may the hand of the Lord grant your request. Wherever you may put your left hand, may His help accompany you" (A nuptial blessing composed by St Ephrem).

What confidence on the part of God to entrust a being, a destiny, to our fragile hands! Only a love that is grafted to the love of God can assume such responsibility. "Do you know whether you will not save your face-to-face?" This question-answer is the sword that slays the individual, the one who is isolated, the "for self." According to St John Chrysostom, a true husband does not hesitate to die for his wife; "you are more precious than my soul," he tells her. In his treatise titled *On the Veil of Moses,* James of Sarug (fifth or sixth century) asks: "What husband, aside from the Lord, ever died for his spouse, and what bride has ever chosen a

[58]There is an infinite distance between, on the one hand, modern "banquets" with their "revelry" and restlessness from which love, deeply wounded, departs and, on the other hand, the wisdom of initiation into the sacramental mysteries.

crucified as spouse? It was man and wife who provided the
occasion to outline this mystery of which they were the
shadow and the prefiguration. [In his story on the creation
of man] Moses gave expression to this great mystery, hiding
it under a veil. The Apostle revealed its splendor to the
entire world, and the words of Moses, 'from being two they
have become one,' were thereby elucidated."[59]

After the Service of Crowning, the reader reads verse 4
of Psalm 20 (21): "Thou hast set upon their heads crowns
of precious stones." Adorned with this symbol, the spouses
listen to the reading of the Epistle to the Ephesians (5:20-33)
and the Gospel according to John (2:1-11). The inexhaustible
richness of the texts invoked converges toward what is essential: the eucharistic nature of nuptial love. The Chaldean rite
affirms this is a fortunate manner: "In his nuptial chamber,
the spouse is like the tree of life in the Church. Its fruits are
nourishing, its leaves bear healing power." "The bride is
like a cup of pure gold, overflowing with milk[60] and sprinkled
with drops of blood." "May the Trinity abide forever in this
nuptial chamber!"

In relating their love to divine love, the spouses raise it
to the level of the Divine Heart, of which the eucharistic cup
is a vivid reminder. This is suggested by the famous icon of
the Holy Trinity by Rublev. The hidden link between the
miracle of Cana, the cross, and the chalice leads to the ritual
of the common cup.

The Euchologion mentions the blessing of the cup. Since
the eleventh century, the ritual in its great outlines reminds
us of the Liturgy of the Presanctified. According to the
Barberini Codex, the cup was eucharistic.[61] With the Armen-
ians and Ethiopians, marriage was celebrated during the
liturgy. St Simeon of Thessalonica[62] describes the fifteenth-

[59]*La vie spirituelle* (1953). As quoted by Dom O. Rousseau in *Le mariage
dans les Eglises d'Orient*, p .13-15.

[60]Some ancient eucharistic rites included the blessing of a cup of milk.

[61]Tertullian notes in his day that the nuptial blessing was given during the
Mass; for a more recent period, the Orthodox canonical collection states that
"marriage is celebrated after the Liturgy" (*Kormchaia Kniga*).

[62]*De septem sacramentis, Against the Heresies and on the Divine Temple*,
chap. 282, PG 155:512-513, trans. John Meyendorff, in *Marriage: An Orthodox
Perspective* (New York, 1975), p. 124-25.

century usage: "The priest takes the holy chalice with the
Presanctified Gifts and exclaims: 'The Presanctified holy
Things for the Holy.' . . . He gives communion to the bridal
pair . . . For Holy Communion is the perfection and the seal
of marriage . . . After that the priest also gives them to drink
from the common cup." Nowadays the betrothed receive
communion during the morning liturgy. During the sacrament,
only the "common cup" is offered, and thus the spouses drink
from the common cup of life.

This ceremony is followed by the reminder of a procession,
a symbolic summary of the nuptial dance of former times. It is
led by the priest, who joins the hands of bridegroom and
bride. The Armenian ritual clearly explains its significance:
the priest represents God the Creator, and he reproduces His
gesture, "Taking the hand of Eve, God placed it in Adam's
hand." In a letter to his friend Anysius, Gregory of Nazianzus, while excusing himself for not being able to be present
at the wedding feast, said that he would join the hands of the
spouses in thought.

Preceding the spouses, the priest leads them three times
in a circular procession, while the paranymphs (bridesmaids)
hold the crowns above them. The procession is accompanied
by a song borrowed from the Service of the Nativity: "O
Isaiah, dance thy joy" and by the troparion, "O holy
martyrs . . ."

The triple procession is a triple reinforcement of the
symbol of the circle. As the geometric enclosure around
ancient temples and cities, the circle symbolizes eternity and
expresses its power of protection. This is the meaning of the
liturgical processions around the temple; by reproducing the
symbol of eternity, they change mere extension into sacred
space. If sacred, liturgical time corresponds to a nostalgia for
the eternal, then sacred space corresponds to the thirst for the
lost Paradise and anticipates the Kingdom. The pathway of
the nuptial life is no longer a simple itinerary; it is placed
on the road to eternity, and the shared advance of the couple
is therefore like the still point of a turning wheel.

The prayer toward the end asks, "Bless their goings out
and their comings in." The texts of 2 Samuel 3:25, 1 Kings

3:7, Acts 13:24, and Luke 13:24 all refer to the importance that has always been given to "entries."[63] He who knows how to come in and go out "worthily" is master of his destiny.

The concluding prayer descends in time and offers a blessing for a long life and numerous progeny. But the dismissal indicates what is essential to the journey and mentions the names of St Constantine and St Helena, "the equals of the apostles," "who saw in the sky the sign of your Cross."[64] Their royal dignity, placed under the sign of the victorious cross, is a reminder of the royal priesthood of the spouses. But these saints are venerated as "equal to the apostles," for the missionary propagation of the faith. The last note of the Service directs the spouses toward their apostolic task: witnessing to the faith through their life, by their nuptial priesthood.

63In the Divine Liturgy, "the Little Entrance" and "the Great Entrance" dominate the progression of the liturgical action.

64[See *Byzantine Daily Worship*, ed. Joseph Ray and J. de Vinck (1969), p. 690]; the ancient rite had this Troparion.

5.

Sexuality and Nuptial Chastity

The Problem

Human sexuality has never received a satisfactory explanation; perhaps it never will. The very transcendence of the Edenic state accounts for a certain vacillation of thought. To some Church Fathers, sexual differentiation is a result of the Fall.[1] The hypothesis is not convincing. Before the Fall, man was created man-woman, and the nuptial community is clearly willed and blessed by God: "God saw all that He had made; it was very good."

Many statements by the Church Fathers are of a strictly pedagogical nature: "We surmise that married life is useful, because this thought stimulates the impulse toward perfection," Origen says.[2] It is but one step from there to an excessive spiritualization, to angelism, and Origen unwisely made it. The flesh is a visible embarrassment, but it demands a less radical solution.

The Gospel contains no "ethical system." The surprising newness of its judgments arises from the fact that they refer not to moral principles, but to the absolute value of the Kingdom and to the love of the King.[3] The principle of "the

[1] St John of Damascus synthetizes certain opinions of Gregory of Nyssa and Maximus the Confessor (PG 94:1208). In his anthropology, St Gregory of Nyssa moves in the direction of an excessive spiritualization thereby reducing human life to an angelic existence, to pure spirit (*De hominis opificio*, CVII, PG 44:188). In his mature age, St John Chrysostom energetically rejects this theory and reestablishes the doctrinal balance in a masterful manner.

[2] PG 16:509.

[3] See D. de Rougemont, *Comme toi-même* (Appendix I and II) (Paris, Albin Michel, 1961).

Good" is, at the very most, respected; one only *loves* the Good when it is a living person, God; this existential attitude explains all the paradoxes of the Gospel. This is the reason why "the sinful woman" is not "handed over to Satan" (the Pauline pedagogy), but pardoned, "for she has loved much," which means in the context that she has deeply felt her forgiveness and has shown a great love for the Lord. If St Paul, as a shepherd of souls, advises not to associate with "people leading an immoral life," it is to these people that Christ, Lord of souls, addresses some of His most profound utterances.

The hidden meaning of the text about the "eunuchs for the sake of the Kingdom" is very complex, for the demand of the absolute is addressed as much to the married as to the celibate, and for the same reason: "When Christ commands to follow the narrow path, He is not speaking to monks, but to all men . . . It follows that the monk and the layman must attain the same heights . . . ," as St John Chrysostom teaches.[4]

In the well-known words, "the unchaste will not enter the Kingdom," one usually sees a condemnation of adultery. However, according to the Gospel, it is the rich who will not enter the Kingdom. A certain alienation toward one's neighbor can prove to be the greatest unchastity. A contrast is emphasized between the judgment-forgiveness for sins of the flesh and the extreme severity toward faults of the spirit.

The "personal advice" of St Paul on marriage, his manifest misogyny, are in view of the Parousia; since the time is short, cares for the things of this world are condemned. Every desire to please his wife divides man and detracts from the service of the Lord. However, what St Paul asks of widows (1 Tm 5:5, 10), that which is "pleasing to God," namely "to put all her hope in God, persevering in prayer and good works"—is this not perfectly accessible to married women?

Ascetic rigorism that is hostile to the senses tends to treat flesh, Eros, and sin as being identical. But the Church of the Councils has never espoused this mentality. On the subject of obscenity, the Council in Trullo (the Quinisext, 692) specifies that evil resides in impure, carnal thoughts, in the imagina-

---

[4] *In Epist. ad Haebreos Homilia* VII. 4.

tion that renders the spirit "voluntarily knowing and willful," whence the ascetic principle of the "custody of the eyes," the purification of the spirit. At the time of the First Council (Nicea, 325), the extremist ascetic trend wanted to advocate the state of celibacy for priests under the pretext that the liturgical rites and the celebration of the Eucharist are incompatible with nuptial life. It was St Paphnutius, monk and rigorous ascetic, who brought about the decision of the Council to canonize the married state for priests. The Council of Gangra (*ca.* 340) strongly condemns (in Canon IV) all abhorrence of conjugal relations, for "marriage in itself is worthy and without blemish"; thus being sanctified, it is chaste. St Amphilochius, bishop of Iconium (d. 394), proclaims the typically Orthodox view: the estate of marriage and of virginity are both highly honorable, for they are both equally instituted by God.

At the dawn of Christianity, the generous leaven that was cast in the pagan flesh of humanity had to be virgin. The consciousness of the Church took shape and deepened itself under the stimulating tide of heresies. Even so, the approach to meaning, ever more rich and universal, is slow.

One should recognize that the current view does not value marriage properly. As the result of an obscure reprobation,[5] conjugal relations burden the conscience. The famous utterance, *inter feces et urinam nascimur,* outdoes some Old Testament texts in a tiresome and simplistic manner: "I was shapen in iniquity; and in sin did my mother conceive me." It makes one forget that these texts are all set *before the Incarnation;* their use, by force of repetition, distorts the evangelical concept of the flesh and sin. Whence the extreme poverty of the status of sexuality in current teaching. It is only too evident that under its influence many couples live in want of completeness.[6]

Yet, the future of the world depends on a solution tailored to man. It is not "in spite of marriage," but in its fulfillment that spouses live the supernatural and holiness of their union.

[5]The latter rejoins Tolstoy's *Kreutzer Sonata* and its violent denial of all mystical depth of the flesh.
[6]See, for example, *Le conflit vécu,* in *Etudes Carmélitaines* (1936).

Love fulfilled has no history, no literature. The nuptial
kenosis unveils its secret only to the eyes of God and to no
other. Without slipping into the error of ineffective compari-
sons, one should pay serious attention to the balanced teaching
of St John Chrysostom: "the perfect spouses are not inferior
to monks," "they can manifest greater virtues than the
monastics."[7] But certainly, to marry, just as to become a monk,
means to take an absolute risk . . .

The Modern Myth of Sexuality

The "proper sex" of bourgeois mentality has long cultivated
the licentiousness of legalized mating. After the hypocritical
Victorian modesty of the nineteenth century, the collective
letdown, the demystification of sexual taboos, ends in an
unprecedented erotic freedom. Public life is invaded by an
obsessive and tiresome sexuality. Even the conventions of
specialists speak no longer either of love or of Eros, but of
sexuality. We are watching its rising tide. More than ever
the word of St Isaac the Syrian applies: "The world is an
immoral woman drawing to herself all men who esteem her
by coveting her beauty."[8]

Filmed under the "flashbulbs," projected on screens and
posters, the former mystery remains only as provocative, rank
sex, anatomy delivered to a morbid curiosity, quickly sated.
The universal loss of the sacred relegates love to an insignificant neutral zone, to the level of a simple physiological release. A dismal banality is shot through by convulsions like
those of insects electrified for a brief moment. One makes love
without love, without joy, and even without pleasure: a
carnivalesque eroticism, within reach of everyone, devoid of
spirit or finesse. But in the long run, a systematic and perpetual degradation produces a very dangerous drop in erotic
sensibility and excitability and threatens the dulled senses
with premature aging and impotence.[9] The collective eroticism

---

[7] *In Epist. ad Ephesios Homilia* XX, PG 62:147; *In illud, propter fornicationes uxorem*, PG 51:209.

[8] Isaac of Syria (Nineveh), Saying 37.

[9] Denudation, the display of flesh, provokes an unexpected reaction and

of the masses, the dissemination of methods, and the general loss of interest deeply trouble psychiatrists who are beginning to speak of a strange "desexualization" of humanity. The overpopulation of the entire world will perhaps find its solution in nature itself; rendered impotent, it would take revenge for having been profaned. Reduced to the flesh, man risks being struck down by the dwindling of his vital forces, which belong to the spirit.

With the help of generalized psychoanalysis, pansexualism marks the end of the great passions. Both the libertine and the frustrated puritan, hostile to the senses, are equally dehumanized. The new erotic conformity upholds the sexual. Virginity, the most beautiful "jewel in the martyr's crown," joyous value of old, has become a burden. This disregard of virginity—which goes so far as to include the contemptuous term "pathological"—and of its eschatological calling, aggravates the systematic degradation of the partners of the modern emancipation. As the object of a new and joyless religion, "glorified sex" has nothing in common with even ancient religious fetishism, which at least knew the sacred and the mysterious; insignificant in its profanations, it sends away its debauched followers, now sicker than ever.

Modern women's novels[10] are symptomatic of this immodesty that disrobes naturally, democratically, knowing neither mystery nor veil. Nowadays the woman, and even the very young girl, "is not taken" but "lets herself be had," out of boredom, and makes love by the sweat of her brow. It is not the flesh but the spirit that is disintegrating, and the nausea that is found at the end leads nowhere; a soulless body is spread out but does not act. The frightening admission, the key word, *ennui,* appears on each page of this literature, which has neither brilliance nor depth. There is a hidden relationship between satisfaction and death. From satisfaction alone

explains the vogue of striptease; the *veiling* and the slow unveiling which a disillusioned sensuality would wish to continue forever. It is not nudity but what is hidden under the veil that excites modern man who is deeply imbalanced. Indirectly, it is the demand of the "veil" that takes revenge on depravity pushed to the limit.

[10]Françoise Sagan, Pamela Morre, Assia Djebar, *e tutti quanti.*

disgust is always born.[11] Schopenhauer said that one must choose between *ennui* and suffering. *Ennui* is an infernal element, the very essence of Hell, for it is without depth and without solution. This is why in an Office for the afflicted, addressed to the Virgin, she is called "the one who destroys the sinful sadness." There is, then, a sadness that is *sin;* it derives from *ennui* and flows into the despair of *acedia*,[12] a deadly sin according to the ascetics.

Love divorced from the spiritual offers little but the bodies from which the soul is absent, and produces mental havoc. The "for self" becomes "for my pleasure" and denotes an ape-like, degenerate mentality. Sooner or later, all nihilism destroys itself from within with the frightening question, "What for?" And sexual nihilism with, "And then?" The insane and the maniacs are multiplying; how distressing it is to accept their vision as the norm because of their sheer weight of number. The uniform banality causes even Eros to yawn with boredom.[13]

This all too masculine world, where the feminine charism plays no role, where the woman becomes mannish, is increasingly a world without God, for it is without the Mother-Theotokos. God cannot be born therein. It is symptomatic that in this atmosphere incest, homosexuality, and the corruption of children are openly asserted.

On the fringe of the Kinsey reports thrive the erotic snapshots of *The Flanders Roads* (*Routes de Flandres*), the "nymphets" of Nabokov, *The Lovers* (*Les Amants*) of Louis Mallé, *The Tropics* of Henry Miller, *Warrior's Rest* (*Le repos du guerrier*) by Christiane Rochefort, *The Mandarins* (*Les mandarins*) of Simone de Beauvoir, and the self-determined ones from Sartre's suffocating hothouses.[14] This litera-

---

[11]See Gabriel Marcel, *Etre et avoir*, English trans. *Being and Having*, Katherine Ferrar (New York, 1955); Alberto Moravia, *La noia*, English trans. Angus Davidson, *The Empty Canvas* (New York, 1961).

[12]An ascetic term that indicates the ultimate state of spiritual dejection. Life unravels itself in *ennui.*

[13]See Sinclair Lewis, *Babbit* (New York, 1922). *L'année dernière à Marienbad* discovers the boredom at the heart of eroticism.

[14]To the Sartrean statement that "man is condemned to freedom," Merleau-Ponty replies admirably, "Because we are in the world, *we are condemned to*

ture faithfully reflects the modern condition of the soul that assimilates the religious with "sex," enthroning the latter and leading us to the "kingdom of intercourse." The obscene asserts itself over the knowing denial of "sin" and uncovers vice in the very heart of man (*Sade*, by G. Bataille). In an unhallowed world, unmasked, sterile, omnipresent sex establishes itself. Here it is no longer possible to give to love not only an anatomy, but even a face. To a brooding Faulkner, quoting Shakespeare, life is identified as "a tale told by an idiot, full of sound and fury, signifying nothing."

D. H. Lawrence, in other respects a very gifted writer, only manages, in spite of all his efforts, to substitute sexual technique for spiritual elevation. The failure of erotic literature is telling. It is to Dostoevsky's credit to have understood the erotic principle in its ultimate depth. When Fyodor Karamazov concludes the account of his debaucheries with the story of the sacrilege committed on a miraculous icon of the Virgin, he gives the key to the riddle. Likewise in his confession, Stavrogin from *The Devils* (*The Possessed*) states that he has indulged in sexuality without finding any carnal pleasure in it. He quickly moves beyond this and makes a fatal turn toward sexual pleasure of a more refined nature. At the height of his infamy, in the horror of the crime that he has just committed, his mind is clear enough to contemplate the despair of a pure and innocent child whom he seduces, and who confides to him that "she has killed God." Dostoevsky shows a metaphysical element in concupiscence that surpasses the psychic and the carnal; the dead end to which it leads is essentially spiritual and religious.

The darker the night, the more brightly the stars sparkle. True and immortal values are better defined against a somber background. It is perfectly clear today that the vocation to virginity must be something other than a frustration: it is the *gift* of man to God. What is offered as a sacrifice, *human love*, is also a gift, founded in the same ascendancy to God. A balanced asceticism helps one understand that the life of the body and the soul, in celibacy as well as in married life,

meaning" (*Phenomenology of Perception*, trans. Colin Smith, London, 1962), p. xix.

is an art of the spirit; chastity stands at the beginning of these two expressions of an integral Christian humanism, turned toward the End.

But how symptomatic it is of the still pretheological state of marriage, that there is no archetype of the nuptial being! To take the marriage of St Joseph and Mary is clearly insufficient for this task. Abstinence from sex represses Eros without transfiguring it. Spouses, in order to be holy, must be resourceful even in this day . . .

Chastity

Modern depth psychology (Jung) distinguishes the energy of sex from sexual energy. The human being is a sexual totality; one is man or woman in every fiber of one's being. The energy of sex is a creative force proceeding from the spirit; it is only in penetrating the psychological domain that this force is partially transformed into sexual energy. Ascetic mastery during the course of this transformation is crucial for the destiny of the person.

In nuptial life, sexuality reveals its symbolic meaning: while passionately seeking unity, the one flesh, it goes beyond itself and wakens the thirst for realities that it only foreshadows and symbolizes, a single being. Love invites one to an encounter in the emotions of the body, but only the spiritual can achieve this. The emotional agitation, the discontinuity at the moment of pleasure, imprisons the human being, snatches him from the encounter, opens up an immediate and vertiginous distance. After the initial paroxysm comes solitude, after impulsive attraction, withdrawal. All the charismatic powers of love, all the tenderness of Eros and its quest for the other, must be called into play to fill the void. This is the transcendence of the "for self" toward the pure and transparent presence of the one toward the other. It is clear that the process is entirely positive, oriented toward the chaste integrity of being.

The concept of chastity, *sophrosyne,* points out above all a spiritual quality, complete "knowledge," the power of the integrity and of the integration of all the elements of life. In 1 Timothy 2:15, St Paul speaks of salvation "by means of chastity." The Greek text has *meta sophrosynes*, "by means of the integration of all the elements of the human being into a whole that is virginal," an event that is essentially inward in relation to the spirit. In the direct sense, it is the eschato-logical orientation toward the world to come, where "men will be like angels." An understanding of this text, "salvation through childbearing by means of chastity," that would place it in a functional, instead of an ontological, dimension would be a serious misunderstanding. Transcending the cycle of procreation, the virginal itself is engendered in view of the Parousia. Likewise in marriage, if the reproductive cycle con-tinues life by a series of deaths, this very cycle is saved "by means of chastity," which renders motherhood in all its forms a giving birth to the New Age; the "sacrament of love" is the sacrament of the world to come.[15] This is why the personal-istic aspect of nuptial love alone is decisive. Both the fertile and the childless couple go beyond the functional, the instinc-tive, and the passions for the same reason and personalize, virginize the flesh, integrated down to its completely spiritual depth, down to the reconstitution of the chaste being. The goal of procreation serves the species and reduces love to an instru-mental and utilitarian sexuality. Certainly, the personalistic concept of marriage is an ultimate, aristocratic elevation of the spirit, and it stumbles over the democratization of truths by the masses, and also by its leaders, for it is easier for them to place themselves at the level of the multitude and to reduce marriage to reproductive sexuality. The question of the Grand Inquisitor (in Dostoevsky) again becomes most current: Are the majority of married people not reduced to the condition of soil in order to produce a minority of virgins-gods?

Sexuality is surpassed by its own symbolics; as a symbol of unity, it transcends itself toward the spiritual integrity of the one being. It is only there that marriage rejoins monasti-cism, where the two are united in the eschatological repre-sentation of the Kingdom. On the other hand, the sociological

---

[15]Isaiah (26:18) speaks of this eschatological giving birth to "the spirit of salvation."

concept (procreation) separates and contrasts the two estates.

Monks and married people, the diamond-cutters of heavenly stones, create chastity, bring creation to perfection. We see this in the Pauline dialectic on the subject of circumcision (Rm 2:26-29). St Paul places it on the spiritual plane and outlines a perspective identical to the dialectic of chastity. Their profound relationship justifies a transfer of terms:

> If therefore the uncircumcised [the physiologically nonvirgin] obeys the commandments of the Law [observes the chastity of the spirit], surely that makes up for not being circumcised? The man who keeps the Law [an interior conformation that transcends nature], even though he has not been physically circumcised, is a living condemnation of the way you disobey the Law . . . ["you" designates here the case of the foolish virgins of the parable in which physical virginity is useless]. The Jew [the inwardly virgin, the one whose spirit is virginal] is not the one who looks like a Jew [physically]; and circumcision [virginity] is not that which is visible *in the flesh.* The real Jew is the one who is *inwardly* a Jew [the chaste spirit]; and the real circumcision *is in the heart,* something not of the letter but of the spirit. A Jew like that may not be praised by man, but he will be praised by God.

This praise is given in advance, at the time of the "Service of Crowning" in the sacrament of marriage. In his commentary on Psalm 147, St Augustine states, "Virginity of the flesh belongs to a few; virginity of the heart must be the concern of all."

*   *   *

As long as psychoanalysis confines itself to contend with the irrational and the subconscious by the sole light of reason, it will remain unproductive. One may well consider sin and sickness, fasting and a vegetarian diet, asceticism and sports hygiene to be identical; such treatment falls far short of the power to command ("Rise, go and sin no more"), whether it be directly ("today you will be with me in paradise") or by degrees ("be perfect as your Father in heaven is perfect"). In order to change the very nature of man, one should turn to charismatic means and to the sacramental power of absolution. To be sure, the office of a psychiatrist is not a sanctuary, but a Christian psychiatrist knows the limits of his science and what extends and completes it under the action of grace.

The asceticism of the great spiritual men presents all the elements of what is called sublimation (Freudian) or metamorphosis (Jungian): a progressive elevation in which all that is "sublimated" is drawn and absorbed into a higher sphere. This is the heart of the transfiguration where nothing is either eradicated or suppressed, but where everything is deeply stirred and given a new direction. But in this ascension only asceticism knows its summit, the Sublime and the Most-High.

In the course of the ascent, the sexual energy is freed from pure animality; it becomes human, it is inserted qualitatively into the spiritual. It becomes less and less disordered, losing its blind seductive force while bestowing on man its ascending dynamism. Love penetrates to the very root of instinct and transubstantiates the natural: "Love changes the very essence of things," St John Chrysostom says. It grafts the empirical finalities into the finalities created by the Spirit: it guides and directs everything toward the height, toward the Most-High.

Under the grace of the sacrament, the sexual life is lived without causing the slightest decline of the inner life. Through its symbolism, it becomes a pure source of immaterial joy: "Everything that is perfect in its species must rise above its species, become something else, an incomparable being," Goethe says.

Every one of the sayings of Christ will germinate at the right time, like a grain fallen into the soil. Their hidden meaning inspires those to whom it is given to be men to the end, to complete the entire measure of human conditions "by means of chastity." The prodigal son has at last felt the breath of the Spirit ("he arises and goes to his father"); this movement marks a new age in the destiny of the world. Delighted, man contemplates the immensity of the thought of God about him. God wants to be glorified by His creation,

and this is why the discourse of Jesus on marriage ends with
the statement, "He who can accept this word, let him accept
it!..."

The Apostle Paul is deeply affected by the law of irrational resistance: "I do not understand what I do." The
conscience is hindered by the subconscious which never obeys
direct orders or given and imposed imperatives. The imagination plays an important role here. It nourishes art, embodies
an image in stone, color, sound. But art never creates a living
object, as the myth of Galatea tells us. Likewise, abstract
principles and a prescriptive morality are ineffective. Imagination and its Eros will always demand an incarnate image, a
living icon, a saint. More than ever, an ascetic culture of the
imagination is indispensable. A Dostoevsky, a Bernanos
descend into the darkness, but their imagination is forever
obedient to the image of Christ. An iconographic education
acquaints one with true beauty, teaches the contemplation of
mysteries. It is the soul that is the form of the body's beauty,
and in the beauty of the soul, it is the image of God that
delights us.[16] St John Climacus teaches the chastity of the
imagination by describing the attitude of an ascetic[17] who, on
seeing the beauty of a naked woman, "thereupon glorified the
Creator; and from that one look, he was moved to the love
of God and to a fountain of tears. Such a person . . . has
risen immortal before the general resurrection."[18]

With the intervention of consciousness, concupiscence
enters the sexual life. Indeed, where consciousness is absent,
moral judgment is not exercised, having no point of applica-
tion. Before sin and the Law that reveals it, men were clothed
with their nudity "without shame"; afterward they dress in
modesty, being conscious of the Fall. The instincts no longer
"lie at the door" (Gn 4:7); they have entered the enlightened
field of consciousness.

---

[16]"The paradise of the gnostic believer is his own body, and likewise the
hell of the man who possesses neither faith nor gnosis is his own body."
Quoted by H. Corbin, *Terre céleste et corps de résurrection*, p. 161.

[17]Namely St Nonnus of Edessa, Bishop of Heliopolis, while watching the
beautiful dancing girl Pelagia, who herself became a saint.

[18]*The Ladder of Divine Ascent*, PG 88:893, trans. Lazarus Moore (Boston,
1978), p. 113.

From its root (the part of the word in italics), the word con-*cupiscentia*, epi-*thumia*, Be-*gierde*, signifies the unconscious life of nature. Animals have no concupiscence; they have instinct regulated by nature, and nature is pure. But the prepositions "con," "epi," and "Be," mark the intervention of reason, human consciousness. It is not the "stomach," the unconscious, that defiles man, but that which comes out of his heart, symbolic of a conscious psychic activity. "It is from the heart that proceed evil thoughts, adulteries, fornications. These are the things that defile man." The sin of adultery resides in the willed, covetous gaze. It is the "perverse spirit" that is the source of sexual depravity in paganism; the imagination is perverse when man is conscious of it and consenting. According to the ascetics, then, it is through the imagination that the demons have access to the mind of man; it is by means of the imagination that they exercise their power of temptation. One understands this when one knows that the imagination is directly linked to the emotional life and the latter to Eros and to sensuality. An erotic imagination corrupts the mind, for it revels in impure images without recognizing either limits or endings—this is the unquenchable thirst of Hell. This is why Clement of Rome perceives a sign of perfection when a brother (a Christian) while gazing at his sister (a Christian woman) does not think of the feminine gender as such. "O singular woman, you are the entire species for me," the poet says, expressing "the unique" of nuptial ascesis.

It is here that spiritual attentiveness, prayer, and grace are the only effective weapons. Chastity is the imagination totally purified and under control. The story of Tobias tells this and describes the victory of chastity over the demonic element of concupiscence. It is an amazing Old Testament anticipation of the Christian sacrament of marriage.

Guided by the archangel Raphael, Tobias meets a girl who has had seven husbands, all killed by Asmodeus (the demon of concupiscence). The symbolism is clear: the bridegrooms are possessed by the demonic element of concupiscence and their death shows the deadly character of this passion. The girl, on the other hand, represents chastity: "Lord, you know that I have remained pure," she repeats in her prayers, thus drawing the spiritual protection of the angel.

Tobias "fell so deeply in love with her that he could no longer call his heart his own." He marries Sarah and the angel commands him to cense the nuptial chamber, the transparent symbol of purification and prayer-offering. And "before you sleep with Sarah, arise both of you and call upon the Lord of heaven who will have mercy on you and save you." The demonic spell is broken by the mutual chastity of Tobias and Sarah. Asmodeus is defeated; concupiscence is destroyed at its very root by heavenly protection. (In Hebrew, Raphael signifies a *"healing from God."*) This healing is none other than *chastity*, present in all true love when it is kindled by the "consuming fire of the Eternal." The prayer of Tobias and Sarah is permeated by it: "Lord, I do not take my sister here for any lustful motive [blind passion], but in singleness of heart [the fullness saturated with the Spirit]." And she says *amen* with him.

Birth Control: The Problem of Limiting Births

In the age of the Church Fathers, the problem of birth control was never raised. There are no canons that deal with it. The ancient collections of penitential discipline are no longer entirely applicable; moreover, they say nothing on the subject.[19] To invoke Old Testament texts (for example, the case of Onan, Gn 38:9-10), is to make an exegetical blunder and to be unmindful of the context of ideas of the epoch about the sacred and the taboo, of the Law, and of the messianic expectation. One must therefore start from the *patristic spirit* and not from a precise, inexistent teaching.

It is perfectly clear that one must avoid all complicity with decadent morals. But one must equally steer away from every

---

[19]Alongside the canons that are affiliated with Jewish nomism (strict adherence to Law), there exists an entirely different tradition which suppresses and condemns every notion of basic impurity. Thus, for example, the *Didascalia,* VI; the *Apostolic Constitutions,* VI; St Athanasius, very categorically in his decretal letter, canon II of the Council in Trullo (Quinisext); the *Syntagma* of Athens, IV, 67-77, 598, 611, V. 370 and so forth.

attitude that renounces human responsibility and invokes divine Providence too lightly. Such an attitude has nothing in common with an act of genuine faith. God has given us intelligence and the freedom to choose and to perform conscious deeds, and this gift presupposes the spiritual duty of fully assuming the consequences.

By its intrinsic, eschatological spirit, Orthodoxy teaches that the saints are the true masters of history and that the Church does not have to formulate, organize, and control the temporal. She represents the *theandric* (divine-human) conscience in the world. She addresses herself to the evangelical *metanoia* and hopes to change man into a new creature, to render him charismatic; she exorcizes demonic powers and protects the Gate of life. She discerns among spirits and shows the pathway to ultimate liberations. She does not define the rules of social life and does not prescribe panaceas. Nor does she give ready-made answers to take *the place of free man*. In the image of God, she has an infinite respect for the dignity of man, priest of the royal Priesthood, and puts her confidence in him, expecting from him his own decisions on the plane of the holy and the sacred.

In this manner, affirming the personalistic aspect of marriage, Orthodoxy will always defend the dignity of adult spouses. The Church, the episcopate, the priest, will never refuse counsel when it is sought, but this advice will always be personal and outside all generalized discipline, outside the ethic of the "common good" and the law.

In an article on the concept of sin in Orthodox theology,[20] the priest V. Palachkovsky states, on the subject of methods of contraception: "In the regular practice of the Russian Church, the priests, out of discretion, never ask questions on this subject. . . . In the opinion of the confessors, the entire domain of the relations between husband and wife is too intimate to provoke investigations by the priest. . . . At present, the question is never asked, because, as has been said, the domain of the sexual relations of spouses does not usually become the object of investigations by the Orthodox confessor, the latter

[20]"Le péché dans la théologie orthodoxe," in *Théologie du péché* (a collection of articles), Bibliothèque de théologie (Desclée, 1960), p. 507-8.

not wishing to penetrate the intimacy where the unity of two in one flesh is accomplished and where the presence of a third is superfluous, even when invested with the priesthood and if only by his questions."

The opinion cited expresses the Orthodox attitude very clearly and correctly. The essential fact here is that the episcopate takes very seriously the concept of the royal priesthood of believers and the crowning of the married couple that establishes them in a nuptial priesthood. Man is truly consecrated King, Priest, and Prophet. This dignity cannot remain a game or an abstract title. It is a very definite vocation that calls for great maturity to find its own solution and to form a decision in deference to the free choice of an *adult*. The whole person *lives* his eternal destiny between his conscience and the eyes of God. No third party may intervene. Married love is not the means but the supreme end, a source of holiness. All relationship of teacher to student is to be totally excluded. The words of St Paul, "This is a great mystery," are the promotion to the coming of age, the adulthood, of the spouses and of their love.

What is most important—and it is here that the Orthodox spirit is most decisive—is *the question of the spiritual age*. The couple passes through a maturation that finds an appropriate solution at each "age" of the nuptial life, one that is intolerant of any general formula, of all submission to the concept of the "common good." Nuptial asceticism, nourished by the full life of the Church, draws from itself the necessary mastery to choose and to judge a situation in agreement with the spiritual age of the couple and the spouses' harmonious growth in charisms. At the most, the Church offers only elements for a basis of judgment. She exerts no constraint; her task is to free man from all forms of enslavement in order to make him a free citizen of the Kingdom. As soon as the sociological and finalistic notion of procreation is set aside, a solution arises from the inventive art of the *magnus amor* and from its protecting grace.

In a great number of marriages, the fear of pregnancy brings rise to a dread that threatens all possible harmony. The unplanned child, the child-intruder, unbalances every structure that is already frail. To this is added a feeling of panic in the face of overpopulation. For lack of finding another aim, another meaning to the sexual act than that of procreation, the official teaching becomes inflexible; its doctrinal principles grow harsh. But the nobility of the believing couple consists precisely in drawing from sexuality something other than what links them to the animal world.

The current teaching brings up the inevitable question: can one truly and honestly distinguish, for example, among the computation of fertile days and other contraceptive methods the one that would be able to assure a specific time of fertility in an infallible manner? The distinction between a complete and an incomplete act is grossly materialistic. The teaching formulated by celibates imprisons couples in a casuistry of methods, and forces them to discover tricks in order to dodge and escape the letter of the official doctrine. The latter then with reason views them as "defective" and "irresponsible," as more or less wayward adolescents. The disasters that ensue are overwhelming. One must frankly admit that if the Ogino-Knauss or the Schmulder method is accepted, the boundary between what is authorized and what is not, between what is "natural" or "unnatural," almost disappears, becomes very imprecise and blurred. The Hindu technique in the *Upanishads* and the Tantric writings known as *vajrolî mudrâ* is a mastery that may fall into a category, perhaps surprisingly, of moral theology: the "conjugal embrace." But it is clear that one cannot be deluded by such deceit.[21] The act that becomes "safe" by means of a computation of days or by mastery of the will is in every instance not *natural*, unless one plays with words. Mental contraceptives derive from casuistry, which is neither a spiritual nor a mature solution. In the presence of *interdiction*, every solution is mediated or fraudulent. Even abstinence, when it is imposed and not freely desired and

---

[21]The "Dynam Institute" of Paul Chanson proposes "a technique based on educating the reflexes, which allows one to prolong sexual intercourse and to bring it to a conclusion without arriving at ejaculation." This enterprise calls itself "catholic" and is the logical consequence of a certain pastoral theology. In order to avoid "frauds against nature," one defrauds the system of reflexes in order to be clear with the letter of the law. In reality, this is more than a fraud against nature; it is a perversion of the spirit.

accepted, carries but a deceptive appearance of spirituality and is fraught with conflicts that destroy the balance.

According to a certain moral theology, when the intention of limiting birth is right, the method can be illicit if it is contrary to "nature." But where is the reference point? The Ogino method puts one in accordance with the law, but in this case it is the law itself that is cheating. The problem is not one of methods, but of the spirit with which one employs the methods. Assuredly, the problem is one of the spirit. Every subterfuge falsely reassures the conscience, and wounds love.

Voluntary procreation is more noble than what is due blindly to chance, more often than not unforeseen and un-wanted. If one accepts painless childbirth, there is no reason not to accept a time of temporary sterility, when a birth would pose a serious problem and where love, filled with anguish and anxiety, lives in an atmosphere where it runs the risk of dying. One cannot compel a woman to bring forth. Procreation can only be the reflected creation of free beings who have prepared themselves by prayer. In order that the child be freely wanted, it is essential that the possibility of not having it be given. Between unconscious "proliferation" and forced and imposed continence, the solution must in no way threaten the nuptial communion. With animals, the instinctive sexual life (the rut) carries on fecundation and reduces all sexual manifestation to the moment prescribed by nature. With man, the order is entirely different and all reduction of Eros to procreation lowers it to the animal level. Human love raises the physiological to the level of the reciprocal gift of the spirit and enriches the totality of life with its harmonics. Love includes procreation, but the latter neither defines it nor in any way depletes it, and it is man who makes the decision with his conscience sovereignly free, before God and before the mystery of love.

It is perfectly clear that one cannot purely and simply recommend contraceptive techniques; the most deserving solution lies in spiritual mastery. But man must uplift him-self progressively toward this mastery and do it *freely*. The spouses are "subjects" who respect each other as responsible persons, free to choose their destiny and their art of loving one another.

The true solution will never be easy or mechanical or lazy. Painless childbirth in no way diminishes the total gift; it includes the risk of losing life, certainly the acceptance of spiritual pain. At the hour of its maturity, love transcends all regulation, every technique, all prescription imposed from without and reaches the crucial plane: faithful to its vocation, it cannot avoid the summit of love crucified.

*   *   *

The secularized State favors a laicism that is latently atheist, where the person is but a perfected animal supplied with techniques and recipes. Such perfection leads to neurosis, a profound lack of harmony with self. The human solution can only come from a religious mentality that posits the sacredness of life, initiates a wholesome reflection on the spiritual relationships between the two sexes, and offers ultimate freedoms. The education of adolescents and of the human masses must include a recognition of the *positive and mystical value of chastity.* There exist no problems for a being whose spiritual structure is chaste: he does not choose, but lives, love "supernaturally naturally."

The one who asks for permission, authorizations, and methods proves thereby that he is still an adolescent and does not yet have a right to them. "Morality" has little to say here, for it is the person who is at stake, and there exist no two identical persons in the world. The one who is immature and is satisfied with *a priori* ethics does not transcend the level of the herd, and may find adequate directives therein. But on the level of the person, nothing can be imposed on love. Love knows no moral norms. It knows normative and spiritual values where freedom and inspiration prevail; it is love that discovers these and is nourished by their revelations. Pedagogy abdicates at the threshold of the mystery where love actualizes and engenders the person for eternity. The evangelical manner of abolishing the Law is to accomplish it by fulfilling it. In the nuptial ministry, love skirts the edge of the abyss, but also attains those heights from which life springs up for the Kingdom.

6.

The Institution

Marriage in Eastern Canon Law

The Council of Jerusalem ruled on questions dealing with Christians of Jewish origin. And in his Epistles, St Paul touches on the management of assemblies, the qualities required of bishops, and the use of charisms. During the first three centuries, the Church used the customary law found in the *Didache* (from the end of the first century), the *Apostolic Tradition* of Hippolytus of Rome (beginning of the third century), the *Syriac Didascalia* (about 250), and the *Constitutions of the Apostles* (about 380). The fourth century opened the era of the regular Councils, and toward the sixth century the Canon Law of the Byzantine Church was already created.

For legislation regarding marriage, the decrees of the following Councils are important: the Council of Chalcedon (Canons 14 and 16), the Quinisext Council of 692, the Council of Nicaea of about 787, the Photian Synods of 861 and 879, and the Council of 920. One should also add the canonic collections of the local Synods, the 85 Apostolic Canons, excerpts from patristic writings, and the texts of the Eastern Patriarchs. Civil legislation should also be taken into account: the *Novellae* of Justinian, the codification of the emperors of the ninth and tenth centuries, the *Ecloga* of Leo III and his son Constantine, the *Procheiron* of Basil I, the *Epanagoge* (879-886), the *Basilica* (888-890) under Leo VI the Wise, and the *Novellae* of Leo VI and Alexius I Comnenus.

The Nomocanons systematize and bring together the texts: hence, the Nomocanon of John III Scholasticus (end of the sixth century) and the *Nomocanon in XIV Titles* (629, completed by Photius in 883), which became official in Byzantium in 920.

In the twelfth century, commentaries on Byzantine law were composed by Alexios Aristenos, John Zonaras, and Theodore Balsamon. In 1335, Matthew Blastares made a collection of it in his alphabetical *Syntagma*. Finally, in 1350 (1354?) Harmenopoulos composed his canonical collection under the title *Hexabiblos*.

Due to the efforts of the Athonite monks, a collection published in Leipzig in 1802 and in Athens in 1841 became the foundation of Canon Law in the present Orthodox Church, under the title of *Pedalion* ("Rudder"). Patriarchal ordinances continue to interpret it and constitute, among other things, a jurisprudence in matters matrimonial.

The *Nomocanon in XIV Titles* was translated in Russia during the eleventh century. The Synod of 1274 adopted the so-called *Kormchaia Kniga* as the official collection. It was augmented in 1650 by Joseph, Patriarch of Moscow, and by Nikon in 1653, and has remained the official code of law since then. The *Pedalion* was translated in 1839.[1]

*   *   *

Orthodoxy does not have a unified code for all the Churches. Even though this state of affairs presents some inconvenience, a unified Canon Law would presuppose a "single type" as the norm for local Churches, which would be alien to the spirit of Orthodoxy. The profound unity of faith and

[1]Bibliography: Jugie, M., "Le mariage dans l'Eglise gréco-russe," in *Dictionnaire de théologie catholique,* vol. IX, col. 2317; A. Raes, "Le consentement matrimonial dans les rites orientaux," in *Ephémérides liturgiques* (1933-1934); J. Dauvillier, "La formation du mariage dans les Eglises Orientales," in *Revue des Sciences religieuses,* vol. XV, 1935, p. 386; J. Dauvillier and C. de Clercq, *Le mariage en droit canonique oriental* (Paris, 1931).

The works of the Russian canonists Sokolovsky, Suvorov, Krasnozhen, Gorcharov, Zaozersky, Zazykin, Sokolov, and Pavlov; the Serbian, Milash; the Greek, Sakellaropoulos, Christodoulou, Theotokas, Antonidis, and Georgiadis.

worship allows for different forms of expression depending on the local tradition.

The dogmas represent what is immutable in revelation, the canons that which is changeable in the historic forms of Church life. The aim of the canons is to circumscribe the dogmatic essence of an epoch and thereby to help the believers embody it in their lives. Beyond the relative and time-bound forms of the canons, the canonical consciousness seeks in out-dated forms the spirit that gave them life and that is always identical to itself. The *jus divinum* and the *jus humanum* are united in the *jus ecclesiasticum,* which prescribes how dogmas are to be applied to the historic life of the Church.

The Canonical Status of Marriage

The Minister of the Sacrament

The betrothal—*mnesteia*—and the crowning are celebrated simultaneously and form a single ritual. Its essential part is the blessing and the crowning of the espoused by the priest. In Russia, this usage has been firmly established since the seventeenth century but became a decree of the Holy Synod of 1775.

St Ignatius already demanded "the approval of the bishop."[2] Canon VII of Neocaesarea mentions the blessing by the priest. John Chrysostom explains the symbolism of the wedding crowns. According to the Byzantine Euchologion, the Service of Crowning—*akolouthia tou stephanomatos*—is the constituent moment of marriage. "If anyone is married without this blessing, this marriage will be null" (Leo VI, in 895). The synodal decree of Michael of Anchialos (1177) clearly states that it is not the will of the bridal pair but the blessing and the sacrament that make marriage. The rite of crowning does not bring an exchange of assent with it. Joachim, the Patriarch of Moscow (1677), kept a formula of interrogation by the priest.

Thus, the only minister of the sacrament is the priest. Even

[2]*The Epistle to Polycarp,* V. 2.

if the approval of the bishop is required, every priest has indeed the power to celebrate a marriage. Normally it is the priest in the parish of the woman. If the betrothed are *alieni juris,* Byzantine law requests the consent of the parents.

Annulment and Divorce

The East permits divorce as a divine dispensation, using as a basis the texts of Mt 5:32 and 19:9. St Basil[3] is the authority on this question, and he affirms the dissolution of the marriage bond for reason of adultery (of the wife). Civil legislation introduces other causes. The reasons are indicated by established practice: the adultery of the husband or of the wife, the absence or the lack of news from one of the spouses for more than five years, civil death by condemnation. There is also the case where the husband is elevated to the episcopacy and he—or the wife—enters a monastery (at an advanced age). In such cases the marriage is annulled, although the other party does not receive permission to remarry. Since 1877, the tribunal of the Patriarch of Constantinople reserves the right to grant a divorce for other reasons. In Russia, the Synod of Moscow, by decree of April 20, 1918, adds the following reasons: apostasy, a serious illness (leprosy, syphilis, self-mutilation), incurable folly, and the criminal abandonment of one party by the other. Thus the reasons for annulment are: the death of the very matter of the sacrament (love) through adultery, religious death through apostasy, civil death through condemnation, and physical death through absence.

Impediments to Marriage

According to the present law of Constantinople, consanguinity to the seventh degree constitutes an impediment; a

[3]*To Amphilochius, Concerning the Canon (The First Canonical Letter),* PG 32:677; St Epiphanius, *Adversus haereses* II. 1, PG 41:1024. 2.5; Asterius of Amaseia, PG 40:225.

dispensation can be granted for this degree. In Russia, the decree of the Holy Synod of 1810 restricted this impediment to collateral relationship to the fourth degree, following Canon 54 of the Quinisext Council. Adoptive parenthood has the same effect as natural parenthood.

Age

In 1877, the Holy Synod of Constantinople specified the marriage age: eighteen years for men and fourteen years for women. St Basil forbade one to marry a woman over sixty years of age. Nowadays, the restriction no longer applies.

Differences of Faith

In the case of marriage to a believer of another faith, the latter promises to respect the Orthodox faith of the spouse. The children should be nurtured *in the spirit* of the Orthodox Church. The formula is wide and contains no specifics. The canons allow for the marriage to be celebrated before the minister of the other party.

Restrictions Resulting from Ordination to the Priesthood

Priests and deacons cannot contract matrimony after their ordination. Only lectors and cantors are able to marry (Canon VI of the Quinisext Council). For every celibate member of the order of priesthood and also for monks, marriage is allowed only after they return to the lay status.

Remarriage: Second and Subsequent Marriages

Gregory of Nazianzus teaches that "A first marriage is in full conformity with the law [of the Church]; a second marriage is tolerated by indulgence; a third marriage is harmful. A fourth marriage makes one resemble a pig."[4]

Even with respect to remarriage, the Church has always shown a feeling of reservation. The early Church advised priests not to be present at the feast of persons contracting a second marriage. Canon VII of Neocaesarea declares a bigamist to be under penance. A third marriage is merely tolerated. In 920, the Synod of Constantinople declared all fourth marriages null. The restriction with regard to third marriages disappeared and they are tolerated without penance. A fourth marriage remains absolutely forbidden.[5]

Married Love and Divorce

God has certainly not created man for his own glorification. Instead He has created him for his own suffering, for God is Love crucified. To God, man is not even the means: this is why love is possible only where there are two persons, two subjects. It is God who secures their freedom; if man desires it, God makes him a gift of the sacrament and bestows charismatic love upon him. Only renouncing love in the name of freedom, mercy, or compassion is valid; it is in the name of another love. Such love is beyond question, even beyond freedom. When it becomes something other, questions arise.

When society speaks of love, it understands the family: it is a sociological form, duty, law. The family becomes a social position, and nuptial love a satisfying of the sexual instinct. The masters of thought proclaim only trivialities, and speak like philistines. They prefer to discourse on sexuality. However, the moment one touches upon the mystery, every "moral system" seems immoral. Indeed, the social is built upon the slogan *quieta non movere,* "don't disturb what is

---

[4]PG 36:292C.

[5]Marriage cannot be celebrated on the following days: the Eve of Wednesdays, Fridays, Sundays, and of the Liturgical Feasts; the Eve and the Feast of St John the Baptist; the 28th and 29th of August; the Feasts of the Cross, the 13th and 14th of September; the week before Great Lent, during Lent, and the first week after Pascha; the fast of St Peter and of the Assumption; the Christmas-Epiphany season, from the 15th of November to the 7th of January.

undisturbed." In turn, each innovation is immoral in the eyes of "morality."

The present-day emancipations are superficial. They are made in view of an easy, conflict-free eroticism. The ease with which divorce is granted reduces marriage to very little, to a meaningless temporary mating or even to a business transaction or unavowed interests. Millenarian finalism lowers marriage, in turn, to the plane of organized animality. Its one preoccupation is to diminish and limit the havoc done to society. This is "nuptial control." However, love leaves the world when it becomes insignificant, when values are replaced by systems of social coercion.

There has always been a secret link between love (Eros) and death (Thanatos). When the *Song of Songs* declares that "love is as strong as death," it means that the power is the same and that the question of ultimate victory remains unsettled. Love reaches immortality only when it overcomes fragmentation of the person, social censure, surface conflicts, sexuality, and objectification by transcending all constraint on the spirit and its supreme freedom. Marriage does not justify love: it is its grace.

Love is a break in society and in nature. As a break in the economy of the Fall, it is set against the arbitrary because it brings with it ascetic purification and sufferings that are freely accepted. Raised to the order of the spirit, it can perform miracles. If it is not shared or understood, it becomes martyrdom and carries stigmata. It is not a matter of earthly goods, but rather of protecting the divine freedom in man and of protecting his heavenly worth. In the conquest of the other's otherness, love can become agony, without ever losing its grandeur.

The freedom from all constraint, all imposed objectified form, is entirely positive when it is done in order to build up a world of values by means of the complete sacrifice of the "for self." The latter frees man from the last enslavement coming from himself. When man understands that he to himself is a *gift* of God, he is able to offer it to God. "Thine own of thine own we offer unto Thee," the Liturgy says. Moreover, in this offering he places what is loved, giving it back to God in the expansion of his joy. He offers the icon of the beloved countenance to God. It is only from the dimension of the new creation that man is able to understand love.

No minister of the sacrament can fathom the depth behind the Yes pronounced by a person. It often remains a mystery for the person himself. There is no possible, formal human way of verifying and testing the quality of love, its duration, its depth. Nonetheless, in a union contracted out of interest, or imposed under external pressure, in a union between persons who are not inwardly free, the bond has nothing in common with marriage in the mystical and sacred sense of the word. Love, the very matter of the sacrament, is missing or has completely withered.

Real incompatibilities, "mis-loved" people are found very frequently. Nonetheless, the majority of nuptial disagreements are due to some spiritual failure: a refusal to follow the heroic way of life, a rejection of repentance, the evangelical *metanoia*. A person who betrays his love betrays himself. But this need to remain on the level of the spirit can never be formalized or decreed. Love, like martyrdom, cannot be imposed on someone. The promise of fidelity is borne on the deepest realities of human life and on transrational realities. It is not imposed from without but arises from within, from the heart's dimension, and is addressed to the freedom of the spirit like an invitation to a banquet and a call to suffering. The act of faith enters into it, and one's fidelity comes alive in accordance with the integrity of one's faith. Within this mystery no one is judge except God, to whom the promise is made, and the conscience of the one who made the promise. If faith changes, fidelity also changes; it ceases to be a grace and it becomes a constraint.

"In marriage laws, one gives primacy to the common good over the particular." The principle of indissolubility derives from this formula and discloses its secret motivation: a person is entirely subordinated to "the common good." This is the ultimate alienation. However, the Gospel injunction to "lose one's soul in order to find it" means that one must lose it so that the soul, and not the common good, may be saved. And when one gives away one's soul to another, it is done above all not in a utilitarian manner, for one's profit, but because one loves the other; it is love that exhibits the supreme power of changing the content of one's destiny. Never "I love you in order to save you," but always "I save you because I love you." From God's point of view, the soul, unique in itself, is more precious than the world and the common good; the two values cannot be compared.

According to the Gospel, adultery destroys the very reality, the mystical essence, of marriage. If love is the matter of the sacrament—and Justinian declares that matrimony becomes real only through love (*Novella* 74)—the exchange of promises is only a telling sign of the real presence of love. Adultery is an indication that nothing is left of the matter of the sacrament. Divorce is but a declaration about the absence, the disappearance, the destruction of love, and therefore it simply declares that a marriage does not exist. It is analogous to the act of excommunication; it is not a punishment, but a post factum determination of a separation that has already taken place.

In permitting divorce, the Orthodox Church shows its infinite respect for the person and for the sacrament of charismatic love. Nonetheless, if it makes divorce difficult and is clearly stating its reservations about divorce it is because the Church wants to prevent all guilty frivolity and ward off the danger of compromising one's destiny. The Church always shows its trust and recognizes that the adult person is the only judge of his life. The greatness of his life, the greatness of the sacrament, demands it, for married life is the perpetuation of the sacrament and it can never be profaned without incurring an inherent danger, the emptiness of hell.

In terms of what is called the Pauline Privilege (1 Co 7:12-16), the marriage of the nonbaptized may be broken in favor of the one who converts. However, it would seem that St Paul recommends the exact opposite: he allows the one who has not converted to break the marriage. At any rate, in this passage, mystery takes precedence over the law: "the brother and the sister are not bound." While commenting on this passage, St John Chrysostom writes, "it were better if the marriage were to be annulled, and no breach made in godliness."[6] "Salvation is for those who desire it," St Gregory of Nazianzus declares.

Thus the Church recognizes that there are situations in which the nuptial life has lost its sacramental essence and has become a prolonged profanation, which may lead to the soul's perdition. The indissolubility of the bond can provoke lies; by protecting the common good, the private good is sacrificed. In order to protect sociological appearances, the worthy face of the *pater familias*, society has instituted prostitution, with the connivance of the State. It pays the cost of established monogamy. This is perhaps why the Gospel mentions the enigmatic utterance about prostitutes who will be first in the Kingdom . . .

The indissolubility of the bond does not promote love. The question of divorce arises when there is nothing left to save; the bond declared indissoluble at the beginning is already broken, and the law has nothing that can replace grace. The law can neither heal nor restore to life, nor can it say, "Arise, and walk."

We are confronted by a very strange phenomenon. In the Gospels, of all the sins, the emergence of the satanic sin of pride is judged most severely. However, it is nonetheless in sexuality that the moral theologians discover the essential manifestation of original sin, and it is precisely because marriage is reduced to procreation that divorce is condemned. The mystery of love is misunderstood, but the social contract receives the status of an absolute obligation. However, baptismal promises involve and put the fidelity of the believer under the same obligation, and for the same reason. The life of the average Christian is in flagrant contradiction to the dedication of baptism; this state of continued perjury does not at all prevent one from being a member of the Church, in spite of the fearful warnings of St Symeon the New Theologian. The Gospel states that the rich will not enter into the Kingdom of God: in the Church, the broadest highway is open to them.

[6]*Homily XIX on First Corinthians*, PG 61:155, trans. Talbot W. Chambers, *Nicene and Post-Nicene Fathers*, series 1, vol. XII (Grand Rapids, Rept 1977), p. 108.

In the midst of the false claims of modern times, there is a sincere cry, a deep desire for the ultimate realities of existence. One cannot reach these without the freedom of the human spirit, without its maturity which makes of him an adult believer, solely responsible for his destiny. It is only on this plane that he can rediscover the grandeur of faith, destroy the dismal monochrome and the *ennui* of hell, and live his most passionate adventure. Then the flowers open up in the world, and miracles occur . . . He feels under his feet not the sociological sand, but this moving ocean that can be reversed into the depth of heaven and the Kingdom.

Two spirits unite to face together the difficulties and the tragedy of life. Two worlds pool their wealth and their poverty, their history and their eternity. It is the history of humanity beginning with Adam and Eve that is projected into their frail existence. It is the totality of the Masculine and the totality of the Feminine that preside over this birth in love; in this summary of the universal they hope to detect one reply to their expectation, a miracle. This is why every love is always unique, and its promise is like the first sun on the first morning.

Monastic virginity has had the privilege of revealing the absolute value of the human person, of affirming the grandeur of marriage. However, a monk can abandon his monastic state precisely in the name of his person and his free vocation. This is why the same freedom should be offered to the married. The Yes they pronounced is valid only on the condition that they can say No at any moment.

Freely as kings they ascend toward their integrity; it is only at the end of their total freedom that their love transcends this world; it mounts toward its true heart, announces the Kingdom, and reaches the dazzling blaze of its real Transfiguration.

Having reached the end of our investigation, we can ask ourselves whether it was not a poetic idealization removed from the real. Paul Claudel specifies the poetic function well: "You explain nothing, O poet, but through you all things become explainable."[7] It is the poetry of the Fathers of the

[7]*Théâtre* (Paris: Gallimard, 1956), p. 428.

Church that opens the aeonic depths and leads to the flame of things. The poetry of love triumphs over the day-to-day real, over the ponderous seriousness of the theoreticians, over infernal *ennui*, over the prose of the unlivable "good sense." It speaks the language of the "fools of God"—the God-intoxicated—those who breathe the insufflations of the Spirit and who add fire to fire; likewise, the language of those who let their own death mature inside them like a fruit of the Resurrection, and finally of those whose human love leads to the love of God. "The love of God and the love of man are not two loves," Maximus the Confessor states, "but two aspects of the same unifying love."[8]

It is at this level that the choice for or against Christ operates, for "Christ died on the Cross so as to condemn condemnation."[9] One must lose oneself in order to find oneself, and there is salvation only in a communal Adoration, the poetry of which comes to us from the blindingly bright pages of the Book of Revelation. According to St Irenaeus, Mary is the Earth which has become virgin again so that God could fashion the new Adam from her. Everyone's fiat rejoins hers and discovers chastity.

"God uses patience" and He grants a mysterious delay, for it is up to man "to hasten the day of the Lord," to place himself already inside the Parousia like the angels of salvation and "to understand how the One who is present is always coming" (St Gregory of Nyssa). It is a question of the "intensity of our love," of those births through faith that are proper to man and woman and that lead the world in the direction of the Lord. A secret germination prepares "the springtime of the Spirit,"[10] the Banquet where the nuptial love of God and of His people is finally realized in every human soul. The joy of Easter resounds in new harmonics; against demonic pessimism and the wear of time stand the words of Origen, "The Church is full of the Trinity."[11] Since Pentecost, the Church is filled with saints . . .

[8]*Epistolae,* PG 91:401d.
[9]*Quaestiones ad Thalassium,* PG 90:408D.
[10]Gregory of Nyssa, PG 36:620D.
[11]*Selecta in Psalmos* 23.1, PG 12:2165.